# KASPAR

*Kaspar* is the most extraordinary and impressive play to date by Peter Handke, the young Austrian-born poet and playwright. First staged in Germany in 1968, it was hailed by Max Frisch as 'the play of the decade'. The central character is Kaspar, a figure based on the historical Kaspar Hauser, an autistic adolescent, who is guided and taught until he speaks 'normally', by the voices of unseen prompters. As the words begin to coincide with reality, Kaspar learns to manipulate both. In the latter part of the play the tension between the individual and 'the others' is further expressed through the image of the original Kaspar surrounded by a host of identical 'Kaspars'.

Having chosen language as a vehicle, Peter Handke explores it as a means of oppression – a means of creating artificial uniformity by teaching people to comprehend the world only in terms of the speech patterns they are given.

*The photograph on the front of the cover shows Wolf Red as Kaspar in the 1968 production of the play at the Theater am Turm, Frankfurt-am-Main; it is reproduced by courtesy of Gunter Englert. The photograph of Peter Handke on the back of the cover is reproduced by courtesy of Suhrkamp Verlag.*

of sentences against inverted sentences about the world? Or: Can Kaspar, by inverting inverted sentences, at least avoid the false appearance of rightness?

16 phase Who is Kaspar now? Kaspar, who is now Kaspar? What is now, Kaspar? What is now Kaspar, Kaspar?

1 phase Can Kaspar, the owner of one sentence, begin and begin to do something with this sentence?

2 phase Can Kaspar do something against other sentences with his sentence?

3 phase Can Kaspar at least hold his own against other sentences with his sentence?

4 phase Can Kaspar defend himself from other sentences and keep quiet even though other sentences prod him to speak?

5 phase Can Kaspar only become aware of what he speaks through speaking?

6 phase Can Kaspar, the owner of sentences, do something with these sentences, not only to other sentences but also to the objects of the other sentences?

7 phase Can Kaspar bring himself into order with sentences about order, or rather, with ordered sentences?

8 phase Can Kaspar, from the order of a single sentence, derive a whole series of sentences, a series that represents a comprehensive order?

9 phase Can Kaspar learn what, in each instance, is the model upon which an infinite number of sentences about order can be based?

10 phase Can Kaspar, with the sentence model he has learned, make the objects accessible to himself or become himself accessible to the objects?

11 phase Can Kaspar, by means of sentences, make his contribution to the great community of sentences?

12 phase Can Kaspar be brought to the point where, with rhyming sentences, he will find rhyme and reason in the objects?

13 phase Can Kaspar put questions to himself?

14 phase Can Kaspar, with uninhibited sentences which he applies to his old inhibited sentences, reverse the inverted world of these sentences?

15 phase Can Kaspar defend himself at least with an inverted world

# KASPAR

'Kaspar' originally published in German © Suhrkamp Verlag, Frankfurt-am-Main, 1967.

First published in Great Britain in 1972
by Eyre Methuen Ltd
11 New Fetter Lane London EC4 P4EE
English translation copyright © 1969 by Farrar, Straus and Giroux Inc
Printed in Great Britain by
Cox & Wyman Ltd
Fakenham, Norfolk

SBN 413 28900 1 (Hardback)
413 28910 9 (Paperback)

Peter Handke

# KASPAR

*Translated by*
MICHAEL ROLOFF

EYRE METHUEN
LONDON

## 16 YEARS

thixtheen years
thoutheast station
whath thould
whath thould
he do
thoutheast station
thixtheen years
whath thould
the fellow
whath thould
he do
thixtheen years
thoutheast station
what thould
he do
the fellow
with hith
thixtheen years

*Ernst Jandl*

The play *Kaspar* does not show how IT REALLY IS or REALLY WAS with Kaspar Hauser. It shows what IS POSSIBLE with someone. It shows how someone can be made to speak through speaking. The play could also be called *speech torture*. To formalize this torture it is suggested that a kind of magic eye be constructed above the ramp. This eye, without however diverting the audience's attention from the events on stage, indicates, by blinking, the degree of vehemence with which the PROTAGONIST is addressed. The more vehemently he defends himself, the more vehemently he is addressed, the more vehemently the magic eye blinks. (Or one might employ a jerking indicator of the kind used on scales for tests of strength in amusement parks.) Although the sense of what the voices addressing the protagonist say should always be completely comprehensible, their manner of speaking should be that of voices which in reality have a technical medium interposed between themselves and the listeners: telephone voices, radio or television announcers' voices, the voice that tells the time on the phone, the voices of automatic answering services of all kinds, the speech mannerisms of sports commentators, of stadium announcers, of narrators in the more endearing cartoons, of announcers of train arrivals and departures, of interviewers, of gym teachers who by the way they speak make their directions correspond to the sequence of the gymnastic movements, of language course records, of policemen as they speak through megaphones at demonstrations, etc., etc. These manners of speaking may all be applied to the text, but only in such a way that they clarify the SENSE or NONSENSE of what is being said. The audience need not be aware which manner of speaking is being used at any given moment, but, etc. At the same time, the miniature scenes should be projected, enlarged, on the back of the stage.

Kaspar (Kasper means clown in German) does not resemble any other comedian; rather, when he comes on stage he resembles Frankenstein's monster (or King Kong).

The front curtain is already drawn. The audience does not see the stage as a representation of a room that exists somewhere, but as a representation of a stage. The stage represents the stage. At first glance, the objects on the stage look theatrical: not because they imitate other objects, but because the way they are situated with respect to one another does not correspond to their usual arrangement in reality. The objects, although genuine (made of wood, steel, cloth, etc), are instantly recognizable as props. They are play objects. They have no history. The audience cannot imagine that, before they came in and saw the stage, some tale had already taken place on it. At most they can imagine that the stage hands have moved objects hither and thither. Nor should the audience be able to imagine that the props on stage will be part of a play that pretends to take place anywhere except on stage: they should recognize at once that they will witness an event that plays only on stage and not in some other reality. They will not experience a story but watch a theatrical event. This event will last until the curtain falls at the end of the piece: because no story will take place, the audience will not be in a position to imagine that there is a sequel to the story. The stage should look something like this: the backdrop of the stage consists of a curtain of the same size and fabric as the front curtain. The folds of the curtain are vertical and plentiful, so the audience has difficulty distinguishing the place where the curtain parts. The wings are bare. The props are in front of the backdrop: they are obviously actors' props. They look new, so the audience won't think they are seeing the representation of a junk shop; and to avoid this possibility, the objects are in their normal positions: the chairs are straight up, the broom is leaning, the cushions lie flat, the drawer is where it belongs in the table. However, so the audience won't think it is seeing the representation of a home-furnishing exhibition, the objects are situated without any obvious relationship to each other; they stand there tastelessly, so the audience recognizes a stage in the objects on display. The chairs stand far from the table, as though they had nothing to do with it; they do not stand at the usual angle to the table or at a normal angle towards each other (they should not, however, give a picture of disorder). The table and its drawer face the audience. Elsewhere on stage there is another table, smaller, lower, with only three legs. Centre stage is empty. Two chairs stand elsewhere, each with a different backrest, one with a cushion, one without. Somewhere else is a sofa with room for almost five persons. Half the sofa (from the vantage point of those sitting in the centre of the auditorium) should be behind the wings, thus indicating backstage. Elsewhere there is a rocking chair. Somewhere else, a broom and shovel, one of them bearing the clearly discernible word STAGE or the name of the theatre. Somewhere else, a waste-paper basket with the same inscription. On the large table, but not in the middle, stands a broad-necked bottle with water in it, and next to it a glass. At the back of the stage is a stylish wardrobe with a large key in the lock. None of the props has any particularly unusual characteristic that might puzzle the beholder. In front, in the centre of the apron, is a microphone.

The first person in the audience to enter the theatre should find the stage lighted softly. Nothing moves on stage. Every theatregoer should have sufficient time to observe each object and grow sick of it or come to want more of it. Finally, the lights are slowly dimmed as usual, an occurrence that might be accompanied by, for example, a continuous muted violin tone ('The tone of the violin is more ample than that of the guitar' – Kaspar). The theatre is dark throughout the play. (While the audience comes in and as they wait for the play to begin, this text might be read softly over the microphones, and repeated over and over.)

**1**

*Behind the backdrop, something stirs. The audience detects this in the movement of the curtain. The movement begins on the left or right of the curtain and continues towards the centre, gradually becoming more vehement and more rapid. The closer the person behind the curtain comes to the centre, the greater the bulge in the curtain. What at first was only a grazing of the curtain becomes, now that the material is obviously pliable, an attempt to break through. The audience realizes more and more clearly that someone wants to get through the curtain on to the stage but has not discovered the slit in the curtain. After several futile tries at the wrong spots – the audience can hear the curtain being thrashed – the person finds the slit that he had not even been looking for. A hand is all one sees at first; the rest of the body slowly follows. The other hand holds on to a hat, so the curtain won't knock it off. With a slight movement, the figure comes on stage, the curtain slipping off it and then falling shut behind it. Kaspar stands on stage.*

**2**

*The audience has the opportunity to observe Kaspar's face and makeup: he simply stands there. His makeup is theatrical. For example, he has on a round, wide-brimmed hat with a band; a light-coloured shirt with a closed collar; a colourful jacket with many (roughly seven) metal buttons; wide trousers; clumsy shoes; on one shoe, for instance, the very long laces have become untied. He looks droll. The colours of his outfit clash with the colours on stage. Only at the second or third glance should the audience realize that his face is a mask; it is a pale colour; it is life-like; it may have been fashioned to fit the face of the actor. It expresses astonishment and confusion. The mask-face is round because the expression of astonishment is more theatrical on round, wide faces. Kaspar need not be tall. He stands there and does not move from the spot. He is the incarnation of astonishment.*

## 3

*He begins to move. One hand still holds the hat. His way of moving is
highly mechanical and artificial. However, he does not move like a
puppet. His peculiar way of moving results from his constantly changing
from one way of moving to another. For example, he takes the first step
with one leg straight out, the other following timorously and 'shaking'.
He might take the next step in the same manner but reverse the order.
With the next step, he throws one leg high in the air and drags the other
leg heavily behind him; the next step, he has both feet flat on the ground;
the next he takes with the wrong foot first, so that with the subsequent
step he must put the other leg far forward to catch up with the first leg;
he takes the next two steps (his pace quickens and he comes close to
toppling over) by placing the right leg on the left and the left leg on the
right, and he almost falls; on the next step, he is unable to get one leg
past the other and steps on it; again, he barely avoids falling; the next
step he takes is so long he almost slips into a split, consequently he must
drag the other leg laboriously after him; in the meantime he has tried to
move the right leg farther forward, but in another direction, so once more
he almost loses his balance; on the next step, which is even more hurried,
he places one foot toe-forward, the other toe-backwards, whereupon he
attempts to align the toe on one foot with the toe on the other, becomes
discombobulated, turns on his axis, and, as the audience has feared all
along, finally falls to the ground. Before this occurs, however, he has not
been walking towards the audience; his walk consists of spirals back and
forth across the stage; it is not so much walking as something between an
imminent fall and convoluted progress, with one hand holding on to the
hat, a hand which remains on his head when he does fall. At the end of his
fall, the audience sees Kaspar sitting on the stage floor in something like a
disorderly lotus-position. He does not move; only the hand holding the
hat becomes autonomous: it gradually lets go of the hat, slips down along
his body, dangling awhile before it too stops. Kaspar just sits there.*

## 4

*He begins to speak. He utters a single sentence over and over:* I want to
be someone like somebody else was once. *He utters the sentence so that
it is obvious that he has no concept of what it means, without expressing*

*anything but that he lacks awareness of the meaning of the sentence. He*
*repeats the sentence several times at regular intervals.*

5

*In the same position on the floor, the lotus position, Kaspar repeats the*
*sentence, now giving it almost every possible kind of expression. He utters*
*it with an expression of perseverance, utters it as a question, exclaims it,*
*scans it as though it were verse. He utters it with an expression of happi-*
*ness, of relief. He hyphenates the sentence. He utters it in anger and with*
*impatience; with extreme fear. He utters it as a greeting, as an invocation*
*in a litany, as an answer to a question, as an order, as an imprecation.*
*Then, in monotone, he sings the sentence. Finally he screams it.*

6

*When this does not get him anywhere, he gets up. First he tries getting up*
*all at once. He fails. Half-way up, he falls down again. On the second*
*attempt he gets almost all the way up, only to fall once more. Now he*
*laboriously draws his legs out from under him, during which process, his*
*toes get caught on the back of his knees. Finally he pries his legs apart with*
*his hands. He stretches out his legs. He looks at his legs. At the same time*
*he bends his knees, drawing them towards himself. Suddenly he is squat-*
*ting. He watches as the floor leaves him. He points with his hand at the*
*floor which is becoming more remote. He utters his sentence with an air of*
*wonderment. Now he is standing upright, turns his head this way and*
*that, towards the objects on stage, and repeats the sentence :* I want to be
someone like somebody else was once.

7

*He begins to walk again, still in an artificial manner, but now more*
*regularly : for example, the feet are turned inward, the knees stiff ; the*
*arms hang slack, as do the fingers. He directs his sentence, not tonelessly*
*yet without expressing anything, at a chair. He directs the sentence,*
*expressing with it that the first chair has not heard him, at the next chair.*
*Walking on, he directs the sentence at the table, expressing with it that*
*neither chair heard him. Still walking, he directs the sentence at the*
*wardrobe, expressing with it that the wardrobe does not hear him. He*

B

*utters the sentence once more in front of the wardrobe, but without expressing anything :* I want to be someone like somebody else was once. *As though by accident, he kicks the wardrobe. Once again he kicks the wardrobe, as though intentionally. He kicks the wardrobe once more : whereupon all the wardrobe doors open, gradually. The audience sees that the wardrobe contains several colourful theatrical costumes. Kaspar does not react to the movement of the wardrobe doors. He has only let himself be pushed back a bit. Now he stands still until the wardrobe doors have stopped moving. He reacts to the open doors with the sentence :* I want to be someone like somebody else was once.


8

*The tri-sectioning of events now sets in : first, Kaspar moves across the stage, now no longer avoiding each object but touching it (and more) ; second, after having done something to each object, Kaspar says his sentence; third, the prompters now begin to speak from all sides, they make Kaspar speak by speaking. The prompters – three persons, say – remain invisible (their voices are perhaps pre-recorded) and speak without undertones or overtones; that is, they speak neither with the usual irony, humour, helpfulness, human warmth, nor with the usual ominousness, dread, incorporeality or supernaturalness – they speak comprehensibly. Over a good amplifying system they speak a text that is not theirs. They do not speak to make sense but to show that they are playing at speaking, and do so with great exertion of their voices even when they speak softly. The following events ensue : the audience sees Kaspar walking from the wardrobe to the sofa and simultaneously hears speaking from all sides.*

*Kaspar goes to the sofa. He discovers the gaps between the cushions. He puts one hand into a gap. He can't extract his hand. To help extract it, he puts his other hand into the gap. He can't extract either hand. He tugs at the sofa. With one tug he gets both hands free but also flings one sofa cushion on to the floor,*

Already you have a sentence with which you can make yourself noticeable. With this sentence you can make yourself noticeable in the dark, so no one will think you are an animal. You have a sentence with which you can tell yourself everything that you *can't* tell others. You can tell yourself *whereupon, after a moment of looking, he utters the sentence :* I want to be someone like somebody else was once.

how it goes with you. You have a sentence with which you can already contradict the same sentence.

*The prompters stop speaking at about the time Kaspar does something to whatever object he happens to be touching : the sofa cushion falls on the floor at the moment the prompters stop speaking ; this functions like a full stop. Kaspar's sentence after each encounter with an object is preceded by a brief pause.*

### 9

*Kaspar walks to the table. He notices the drawer in the table. He tries to turn the knob on the drawer but is unable to. He pulls on the drawer. It comes out a little. He tugs once more at the drawer. The drawer is now askew. He tugs at it once more. The drawer loses hold and falls to the floor. Several objects, such as silverware, a box of matches, and coins, fall out of the drawer. After regarding them for a moment Kaspar says :* I want to be someone like somebody else was once.

The sentence is more useful to you than a word. You can speak a sentence to the end. You can make yourself comfortable with a sentence. You can occupy yourself with a sentence and have gotten several steps further ahead in the meantime. You can make pauses with the sentence. Play off one word against the other. With the sentence you can compare one word with the other. Only with a sentence, not with a word, can you ask leave to speak.

### 10

*Kaspar walks towards a chair. He tries to walk straight ahead even though the chair is in his way. While walking, he shoves the chair ahead in front of him. Still walking, he becomes entangled in the chair. Still*

You can play dumb with the sentence. Assert yourself with the sentence against other sentences. Name everything that gets in your way and move it out of your way. Familiarize yourself with all objects. Make

*lking, he tries to disentangle*
*imself from the chair. At first he*
*becomes more and more*
*dangerously entwined in it, but*
*then, as he is about to surrender*
*to the chair, he becomes free of it*
*just because he was about to give*
*in. He gives the chair a kick, so*
*that it flies off and falls over.*
*After regarding it for a moment:*
I want to be someone like
somebody else was once.

all objects into a sentence with
the sentence. You can make all
objects into *your* sentence.
With this sentence, all objects
belong to you. With this
sentence, all objects are yours.

11

*Kaspar walks towards the small*
*table. The table has three legs.*
*Kaspar lifts the table with one*
*hand and yanks with the other*
*hand on one leg but is unable to*
*pull it out. He turns the leg, first*
*in the wrong direction. He turns*
*it in the right direction and*
*unscrews the leg. He is still*
*holding the table with the other*
*hand. He slowly withdraws the*
*hand. The table rests on his*
*fingertips. He withdraws his*
*fingertips. The table*
*topples over. After regarding it*
*for a moment:* I want to be
someone like somebody else was
once.

To put up resistance. A
sentence to divert you. A
sentence with which you can
tell yourself a story. You have
a sentence which gives you
something to chew on when
you are hungry. A sentence
with which you can pretend you
are crazy: with which you can
go crazy. A sentence to be
crazy with: for remaining crazy.
You have a sentence with which
you can begin to take notice of
yourself: with which you can
divert attention from yourself.
A sentence to take a walk with.
To stumble over. To come to a
halt with in mid-sentence. To
count steps with.

12

*Kaspar walks towards the*
*rocking chair. He walks around*

You have a sentence you can
speak from beginning to end

it. He touches it as though *unintentionally. The chair begins to rock, Kaspar takes a step back. The chair continues to rock. Kaspar takes one step farther back. The rocking chair stops moving. Kaspar takes two steps towards the chair and nudges it with his foot, making it move slightly. When the chair is rocking, he uses his hand to make it rock more. When the chair is rocking more strongly, he uses his foot to make it rock even more. When the rocking chair is rocking even more strongly, he gives it an even stronger shove with his hand, so the rocking chair is now rocking dangerously. He gives it one more kick with his foot. Then, as the rocking chair is about to tip over, though it is still not quite certain whether it will fall or go on rocking, he gives it a little shove with his hand which suffices to tip it over. Kaspar runs off from the turned-over chair. Then he returns, step by step. After regarding it for a moment:* I want to be someone like somebody else was once.

and from end to beginning. You have a sentence to say yea and say nay with. You have a sentence to deny with. You have a sentence with which you can make yourself tired or awake. You have a sentence to blindfold yourself with. You have a sentence to bring order into every disorder: with which you can designate every disorder in comparison to another disorder as a comparative order: with which you can declare every disorder an order: can bring yourself into order: with which you can talk away every disorder. You have a sentence you can take as a model. You have a sentence you can place between yourself and everything else. You are the lucky owner of a sentence which will make every impossible order possible for you and make every possible and real disorder impossible for you: which will exorcize every disorder from you.

## 13

*Kaspar takes a look around. A broom is standing there. He walks to the broom. He draws the broom towards himself with his hand or*

You can no longer visualize anything without the sentence. You are unable to see an object without the sentence. Without

*foot, so that it now leans at a wider angle. He tugs once more at the broom, again increasing the angle. Once more, just a little. The broom begins to slip, and falls. After regarding it for a moment :* I want to be someone like somebody else was once.

the sentence, you cannot put one foot in front of the other. You can remind yourself with the sentence because you uttered the sentence while taking your last step, and you can recall the last step you took because you uttered the sentence.

14

*Kaspar walks towards the one chair that is still upright. He stops in front of it. He remains standing in front of it for the duration of the sentence. Suddenly he sits down. After looking for a moment :* I want to be someone like. *He has obviously been interrupted in mid-sentence.*

You can hear yourself. You become aware. You become aware of yourself with the sentence. You become aware of yourself. You stumble something which interrupts the sentence which makes you aware that you have stumbled upon something. You become aware: you can become aware: you are aware.

15

*Kaspar sits there. He is quiet.*

You learn to stammer with the sentence and with the sentence you learn that you are stammering, and you learn to hear with the sentence and you learn with the sentence that you are hearing, and with the sentence you learn to divide time into time before and time after uttering the sentence, and you learn with the sentence that you are dividing time, just as you learn with the sentence

that you were elsewhere the
last time you uttered the
sentence, just as you learn with
the sentence that you are
elsewhere now, and learn to
speak with the sentence and
learn with the sentence that you
are speaking; and you learn
with the sentence that you are
speaking a sentence, and you
learn with the sentence to speak
another sentence, just as you
learn that there are other
sentences, just as you learn
other sentences, and learn to
learn; and you learn with the
sentence that there is an order
and you learn with the sentence
to learn order.

16

*The stage is blacked out.*
You can still crawl off behind
the sentence: hide: contest it.
The sentence can still mean
anything.

17
*The stage becomes bright. Kaspar
sits there quietly. Nothing
indicates that he is listening. He
is being taught to speak. He
would like to keep his sentence.
His sentence is slowly but surely
exorcized through the speaking of
other sentences. He becomes
confused.*

The sentence doesn't hurt you
yet, not one word. Does hurt
you. Every word does. Hurt,
but you don't know that that
which hurts you is a sentence
that. Sentence hurts you
because you don't know that it
is a sentence. Speaking hurts
you but the speaking does not.

23

Hurt nothing hurts you because
you don't know yet what.
Hurting is everything hurts you
but nothing. Really hurts you
the sentence does. Not hurt you
yet because you don't know
yet that it is. A sentence
although you don't know that
it is a sentence, it hurts you,
because you don't know that it
is a sentence that hurts. You.

I want to be someone like
somebody else was once.

*Kaspar defends himself with his
sentence :*
I want.
I want to be like once.
I want to be someone like once.
Somebody else.
Like a person else.
Somebody.

*He still maintains his sentence :*
I want to be someone like
somebody else was once.

*He defends himself again :*
Was I.
Somebody else like else.
Somebody else someone.
Be like I.
I be I.

You begin, with yourself, you,
are a, sentence you, could form,
of yourself, innumerable,
sentences, you sit, there but,
you don't, know that, you sit
there. You don't sit, there
because you, don't know that,
you sit there you, can form, a
sentence, of yourself, you sit in,
your coat, is buttoned, the belt,
on your, trousers is, too loose,
you have, no shoelace you, have
no, belt your coat, is
unbuttoned, you are not even,
there you, are an un, loosed
shoe, lace. You cannot defend
yourself against any sentence:

The shoelace hurts you. It
does not hurt you because it is
a shoelace but because you lack
the word for it, and the
difference between the tight
and the loose shoelace hurts

Somebody was.
Be one.
I a person.
I want to be else.
Like somebody else somebody.
Once like somebody.
Was somebody.
Like once.
I want to be somebody like.

you because you don't know
the difference between the tight
and the loose shoelace. The
coat hurts you, and the hair
hurts you. You, although you
don't hurt yourself, hurt
yourself. You hurt yourself
because you don't know what is
you. The table hurts you, and
the curtain hurts you. The words
that you hear and the words
that you speak hurt you.
Nothing hurts you because you
don't know what hurting is,
and everything hurts, you don't
know what anything means.
Because you don't know the
name of anything, everything
hurts you even if you don't
know that it hurts you because
you don't know what the word
hurt means:

*The first divergence:*
I want to be like somebody else
like somebody else once was
somebody else.

*He resists more vehemently but
with less success:*
One.
Be.
Somebody.
Was.
Want.
Somebody else.

You hear sentences: something
like your sentence: You
compare something comparable.
You can play off your sentence
against other sentences and
already accomplish something:
such as becoming used to the
open shoelace. You are
becoming used to other
sentences, so that you cannot
do without them any more. You

25

can no longer imagine your
sentence all alone by itself: it
is no longer your sentence
alone: you are already looking
for other sentences. Something
has become impossible:
something else has become
possible:

Somebody else like I like once I
want to be.

*He resists even more vehemently,
but even less successfully:*
Waswant!
Somelike!
Someonce!
Somel!
Besome!
Likeonce!
Elsh!

Where are you sitting? You are
sitting quietly. What are you
speaking? You are speaking
slowly. What are you breathing?
You are breathing regularly.
Where are you speaking? You
are speaking quickly. What are
you breathing? You are
breathing in and out. When are
you sitting? You are sitting
more quietly. Where are you
breathing? You are breathing
more rapidly. When are you
speaking? You are speaking
louder. What are you sitting?
You are breathing. What are you
breathing? You are speaking.
What are you speaking? You
are sitting. Where are you
sitting? You are speaking in
and out:

Olce ime kwas askwike lein.

*The prompters address Kaspar
very vehemently:*

26

| | |
|---|---|
| *Kaspar utters a very long* e. | Order. Put. Lie. Sit. |
| *Kaspar utters an* n *for not quite as long a duration as the* e. | Put. Order. Lie. Sit.<br>Lie. Put. Order. Sit. |
| *Kaspar utters a shorter* s. | Sit. Lie. Put. Order. |
| *Kaspar utters a brief, formally difficult,* r. | Order. Put. Lie. Sit. |
| *Kaspar utters a* p, *and tries to stretch the* p *like the other letters, an endeavour in which he of course fails utterly.* | Put. Order. Sit. Lie.<br>Sit. Lie. Order. Stand. |
| *With great formal difficulties, Kaspar utters a* t. | Stand. Sit. Lie. Order. |
| *With great effort, Kaspar utters a* d. | Lies. Stands. Sits. In order: |
| *Kaspar seeks to produce some kind of sound by means of movements such as stomping his feet, scraping, shoving a chair back and forth, and finally perhaps by scratching on his clothes.* | *The prompters are now speaking calmly, already sure of their success:*<br>Listening?<br>Staying?<br>Opening up?<br>Hear!<br>Remain!!<br>Open up!!! |
| *Kaspar tries with all his strength to produce a single sound. He tries it with his hands and feet. He cannot do it. His strenuous movements become weaker and weaker. Finally he stops moving altogether. Kaspar has finally been silenced. His sentence has* | *The prompters let him mutely exert himself.* |

*been exorcized. Several moments
of quiet.*

18
*Kaspar is made to speak. He is
gradually needled into speaking
through the use of speech
material.*

The table stands. The table fell
over? The chair fell over! The
chair stands? The chair fell
over and stands? The chair fell
over but the table stands. The
table stands or fell over!
Neither the chair fell over nor
the table stands nor the chair
stands nor the table fell over?!
You are sitting on a chair that
fell over:

*Kaspar is still mute.*

The table is a horror for you.
But the chair is no horror
because it is no table. But your
shoelace is a horror because the
broom is no chair. But the
broom is no horror because it
is a table. But the chair is no
horror because it is the table as
well as the shoelace. But the
shoelace is no horror because it
is neither a chair nor a table
nor a broom. But the table is a
horror because it is a table. But
the table, chair, broom, and
shoelace are a horror because
they are called table, chair,
broom, and shoelace. They are
a horror to you because you
don't know what they are
called:

*Kaspar begins to speak:*
Fallen down.
*He begins to speak a little:*
Because.
Often.
Me.
Never.
Least.
Into.
Let.
Me.
Nothing.
Although.
How.
Because mc here at least already.


*He comes closer and closer to uttering a regular sentence:*
Into the hands.
Far and wide.
Or there.
Fell out.
Beat eyes.
No is.
Goes neither home.
To the hole.
Goat eyes.
Rain barrel.
How dark.
Pronounced dead.
If I myself already here at least tell.


Eels. Running.
Boiled. From behind.

*They continue to stuff him with enervating words:* For a wardrobe on which you sit is a chair, or not? Or a chair on which you sit is a wardrobe when it stands on the place of the wardrobe, or not? Or a table which stands on the place of the wardrobe is a chair when you sit on it, or not? Or a chair on which you sit is a wardrobe as soon as it can be opened with a key and clothes hang in it, even if it stands on the place of the table and you can sweep the floor with it; or not?

A table is a word you can apply to the wardrobe, and you have a real wardrobe and a possible table in place of the table, and? And a chair is a word you can apply to the broom, so that you have a real broom and a possible chair in place of the chair, and? And a broom is a word you can apply to the shoelace, and you have a real shoelace and a possible broom in place of the shoelace, and? And a shoelace is a word you can apply to the table, so that you suddenly have neither a table nor a shoelace in place of the table, and?

The chair still hurts you, but the word chair already pleases

Right. Later. Horse.
Never stood. Screams.
Faster. Puss. Thrashing.
Whimpers. The knee.
Back. Crawls.
Hut. At once.
Candle. Hoarfrost. Stretch.
Awaits. Struggles.
Rats. Unique. Worse.
Walked. Living. Farther.
Jumped. Yes. Should.

Entered am chair without rags
on the shoelace, which
meantime talked to death struck
the feet, without broom on the
table, which are standing turned
over some distance from the
wardrobe, scarcely two saving
drops from the curtain.

you. The table still hurts you
but the word table already
pleases you. The wardrobe still
hurts you a little, but the word
wardrobe already pleases you
more. The word shoelace is
beginning to hurt you less
because the word shoelace
pleases you more and more.
The word broom hurts you less the
more the word broom pleases
you. Words no longer hurt you
when the word words pleases
you. The sentences please you
more the more the word
sentence pleases you:

Words and things. Chair and
shoelace. Words without things.
Chair without broom. Things
without words. Table without
thing. Wardrobe without
shoelace. Words without table.
Neither words nor things.
Neither words nor shoelace.
Neither words nor table. Table
and words. Words and chair
without things. Chair without
shoelace without words and
wardrobe. Words and things.

Things without words. Neither
word nor things. Words and
sentences. Sentences:
Sentences: Sentences:

*Kaspar utters a normal sentence:*
That time, when I was still
there, my head never ached as
much, and I was not tormented
the way I am now that I am
here.

*It becomes dark.*

19
*It becomes light, Kaspar slowly
begins to speak:*
After I came in, as I see only
now, I put, as I see only now,
the sofa into disorder,
whereupon, as I see only now,
the wardrobe door with which
I, as I see only now, played, as
I see only now, with my foot,
was left open, whereupon I, as
I see only now, ripped, as I see
only now, the drawer out of the
table, whereupon, as I see only
now, I threw over another
table, thereupon a rocking
chair, as I see only now, also
turned over, as well as a further
chair and broom, as I see only
now, whereupon I walked
towards, as I see only now, the
only chair still standing (as I
see only now) and sat down. I
neither saw anything nor heard
anything, and I felt good. *He*

*gets up.* Now I have got up and noticed at once, not just now, that my shoelace was untied. Because I can speak now I can put the shoelace in order. Ever since I can speak I can bend down to the shoelace in normal fashion. Ever since I can speak I can put everything in order. *He bends down towards the shoelace. He moves one leg forward so as to be able to bend down better towards the shoelace. But because he was standing with the other leg on the shoelace, he stumbles as he moves the leg forward and falls after making a futile attempt to remain upright – for a moment it looks as though he might stop himself, but he doesn't. In the process he also overturns the chair he had been sitting on. After a moment of silence:* Ever since I can speak I can stand up in an orderly manner; but falling only hurts ever since I can speak; but the pain when I fall is half as bad ever since I know that I can speak about the pain; but falling is twice as bad ever since I know that one can speak about my falling; but falling doesn't hurt at all any more ever since I know that I can forget the pain; but the pain never stops at all any more ever since I know that I can feel ashamed of falling.

*Kaspar sets in. He speaks slowly:*

Do remember that and don't forget it!

Do remember that and don't forget it!

Do remember that and don't forget it!

Do remember that and don't forget it!

Do remember that and don't forget it!

Do remember that and don't forget it!

Do remember that and don't forget it!

Do remember that and don't forget it!

Do remember that and don't forget it!

Do remember that and don't forget it!

Do remember that and don't forget it!

Do remember that and don't forget it!

Ever since you can speak an orderly sentence you are beginning to compare everything that you perceive with this orderly sentence, so that the sentence becomes a model. Each object you perceive is that much simpler, the simpler the sentence with which you can describe it: that object is an orderly object about which no further questions remain to be asked after a short simple sentence: an orderly object is one which is entirely clarified with a short simple sentence: all you require for an orderly object is a sentence of three words: an object is orderly when you don't first have to tell a story about it. For an orderly object you don't even require a sentence: for a normal object the word for the object suffices. Stories only begin with abnormal objects. You yourself are normal once you need to tell no more stories about yourself: you are normal once your story is no longer distinguishable from any other story: when no thesis about you provokes an anti-thesis. You should not be able to hide behind a single sentence any more. The sentence about your shoelace and the sentence about you must be alike except for one word: in the end they must be alike to the word.

## 21

*A spotlight follows Kaspar's hand which is slowly approaching the loose shoelace. It follows Kaspar's other hand, which is also approaching the shoelace. He slowly crosses one shoelace over the other. He holds the crossed ends up. He winds one end precisely around the other. He holds up both ends, crossed. He draws the shoelaces together, slowly and deliberately. He elaborately makes a noose with one lace. He places the other lace around the noose. He pulls it through underneath. He draws the noose tight. The first order has been created. The spotlight is extinguished.*

The table stands. With the word table you think of a table which stands: a sentence is not needed any more. The scarf is lying. When the scarf is lying, something is not in order. Why is the scarf lying? The scarf already requires other sentences. Already the scarf has a story: does the scarf have a knot tied at one end, or has someone thrown the scarf on the floor? Was the knot ripped off the scarf? Was someone choked to death with the scarf? The curtain is falling just now: at the word curtain you think of a curtain that is falling just now: a sentence is not needed any more. What is worth striving for is a curtain that is just falling.

## 22

*The spotlight follows Kaspar's hand, which, by pushing up the jacket, approaches the belt, which may be very wide. The spotlight follows Kaspar's other hand, which also moves towards the belt. One hand slips the belt end*

A sentence which demands a question is uncomfortable: you cannot feel at home with such a sentence. What matters is that you form sentences that you can at least feel at ease with. A sentence which

34

*out of very many belt loops. One
hand holds the prong of the
buckle while the other draws the
belt away from the prong. This
hand pulls the belt tight while the
other hand puts the prong
through the next hole. The belt
end, which has become even
longer through the tightening of
the belt, is again passed carefully
through the many loops until the
trousers fit as they should
obviously fit. The spotlight
darkens.*

demands another sentence is
unpretty and uncomfortable.
You need homely sentences:
sentences as furnishings:
sentences which you could
actually save yourself: sentences
which are a luxury. All objects
about which there are still
questions to be asked are
disorderly, unpretty, and
uncomfortable. Every second
sentence (*the words are timed to
coincide with the loops through
which Kaspar is passing the belt*)
is disorderly, unpretty,
uncomfortable, irksome,
ruthless, irresponsible, in bad
taste.

## 23
*The spotlight follows Kaspar's
hand which is buttoning his jacket
from top to bottom. One button is
left over at the bottom. The spot
points to the leftover button, as
does Kaspar's hand. Then it
follows the hand as it unbuttons
the jacket from bottom to top, but
more rapidly than it buttoned it.
Then it follows Kaspar's hand as
it buttons the jacket once more,
even more quickly. This time he
succeeds. The spot and Kaspar's
hands both point to the
bottommost button. Then the
hands release the button. The
spot reveals that everything is in
order. Then it goes out.*

Every object must be the
picture of an object: every
proper table is the picture of a
table. Every house must be the
picture of a house. Every
proper table is (*the words are
timed to coincide with the
buttoning*) orderly, pretty,
comfortable, peaceful,
inconspicuous, useful, in good
taste. Each house (*the words
coincide with the unbuttoning*)
that tumbles, trembles, smells,
burns, is vacant, is haunted is
not a true house. Every
sentence (*the words again
coincide with the buttoning*)
which doesn't disturb, doesn't

threaten, doesn't aim, doesn't
question, doesn't choke,
doesn't want,
doesn't
assert is a
picture of a sentence.

## 24

*The spot shines on Kaspar. It is
obvious that his jacket does not
match his trousers, either in
colour or in style. Kaspar just
stands there.*

A table is a true table when the
picture of the table matches the
table: it is not yet a genuine
table if the picture of the table
alone coincides with the table
whereas the picture of the table
and chair together do not
coincide with the table and
chair. The table is not yet a
true, actual, genuine, right,
correct, orderly, normal, pretty,
even prettier, spectacularly
beautiful table if you yourself
do not fit the table. If the table
is already a picture of a table,
you cannot change it: if you
can't change the table, you
must change yourself: you must
become a picture of yourself
just as you must make the table
into a picture of a table and
every possible sentence into a
picture of a possible sentence.

## 25

*Kaspar puts the stage in order.
While the spotlight follows him
and everything he does, he moves
from one object to the other and*

*His actions are accompanied by
sentences from the prompters. At
first these sentences are adjusted
to Kaspar's movements, until*

corrects whatever harm he has done to it. *Moreover, he puts the objects into their normal relationships towards each other, so that the stage gradually begins to look inhabitable. Kaspar creates his own (three) walls for himself. Each of his steps and movements is something new to which the spotlight calls attention. Occasionally he accompanies his actions with sentences. Every interruption of the action produces an interruption of the sentence. Every repetition of an action produces a repetition of the sentence. As he nears the completion of his task, his actions more and more obey the sentences of the prompters, whereas in the beginning the prompters' sentences adjusted themselves to his actions. First of all, Kaspar rights the chair on which he had been sitting, saying, for example:* I am righting the chair and the chair is standing. *He goes to the second chair and raises it, this time with one hand. The spot shines on the hand, which holds on to a vertical rod on the backrest:* I am putting up the second chair: I can count. The first chair has two rods. The second chair has three rods: I can compare. *He squats down behind the chair and embraces the rods with both hands. He shakes them:* everything that is

*Kaspar's movements gradually begin to adjust to the movement of the sentences. The sentences clarify events on the stage, of course without describing them. There is a choice among the following sentences.*

Everyone is born with a wealth of talents.

Everyone is responsible for his own progress.

Everything that does harm is made harmless.

Everyone puts himself at the service of the cause. Everyone says yes to himself.

Work develops an awareness of duty in everyone.

Each new order creates disorder.

Everyone feels responsible for the smallest mote of dust on the floor.

Whoever possesses nothing replaces his poverty with work.

All suffering is natural.

Every working man must be given leisure time in accordance with his need to replenish the energy expended while working.

Everyone must build his own world.

barred with rods is a chair. *One rod breaks in half. He quickly puts the two halves together again:* Everything that breaks is only a rod in a chair. Everything that can be covered up is only a rod in a chair. *He walks to the large table. This time, before he kneels down, he pulls his trousers up over his knees:* I pull my trousers up over my knees so they won't get dirty. *He quickly picks up what had fallen out of the drawer:* Everything that cuts is only a table knife. Everything that lies face up is a playing card. *He tries picking up a match with his whole hand. He fails. He tries with two fingers and succeeds:* Everything I can't pick up with my whole hand is a match. *He quietly pushes the drawer into the table. He still has the match in his hand. He sees another match on the floor. He picks it up, whereupon the match in his hand drops. He picks it up, whereupon the second match falls out of his hand (the movements are very precise, the spot follows). For the first time he uses his other hand to pick up the match. He holds the two matches in his two fists. He no longer has a hand free to open the drawer. He stands before the drawer. Finally he gives the match from one hand to the other*

Example is a lesson that all men can read.

A foolish consistency is the hobgoblin of little minds.

Good order is the foundation of all things.

A fanatical desire for order does not have to lead to a *coup d'etat*.

Every step extends one's perspective.

That table is a meeting place.

The room informs you about its inhabitant.

An apartment is a prerequisite for an orderly life.

Flowers should stand there as though they had a common centre.

Don't stand if you can sit.

Bending down expends more energy than anything else.

A burden is lighter the closer it is held to the body.

Put only things you don't use often into the top shelves.

Saving means saving energy.

Balance the weight on both arms.

The table won't run away from you.

*hand:* I can hold one hand free. Everything that can move freely is a hand. *He opens the drawer wide, with one hand. He puts the matches in the drawer, pushing the drawer shut with the other hand, whereupon the first hand gets caught in the drawer. He pulls on the caught hand while pushing in with the other hand, exerting himself more and more in both endeavours. Finally he is able to free his hand with one violent pull while the other hand, with one violent push, pushes in the drawer. He does not rub his hand but moves on immediately, righting the rocking chair, which had fallen near the table, almost in one movement with the bang of the drawer as it is shut. Immediately afterward he leans the broom against the wall. Almost before the audience has time to realize it, he is kneeling before the three-legged table replacing the leg, all his movements being rapidly followed by the spotlight. As he moves, he says, also very rapidly:*
Everything that bangs is only a table drawer: everything that burns is only a chapped lip: everything that puts up resistance is only a fallen broom: everything that gets in the way is only a snowdrift: everything that rocks is only a rocking horse: everything that

Always take a fresh look at your work.

Only if you're healthy can you achieve a lot.

Disorder outrages all decent-thinking men.

One of the most beautiful things in life is a well-set table.

The furnishings should complement you.

Apportion your time correctly.

A place for everything and everything in its place.

Happy are those who have steered a middle course.

Nothing is given to you in life.

The fingernails are a special index of order and cleanliness.

Suggest with a friendly smile that you like your work.

What has always been the way you find it, you won't be able to change at once.

Everyone must be able to do everything.

Everyone should be completely absorbed in his work.

Everything that appears to harm you is only in your best interest.

You should feel responsible for the furniture.

dangles is only a punching ball: everything that can't move is only a wardrobe door. *In the meantime he has marched to the wardrobe door and banged it shut. But it won't stay shut. He slams it shut again. It slowly opens again. He pushes it shut. As soon as he lets go of it, it opens up again:* Everything that doesn't close is a wardrobe door. Everything that frightens me is only a wardrobe door. Everything that hits me in the face is only a wardrobe door. Everything that bites me is only a wardrobe door. (*Each of these sentences coincides with Kaspar's attempts to slam or push the door shut.*) *Finally he leaves the wardrobe open. He goes to the sofa, puts it back in order, at the same time shoving it completely on stage. The spotlight precedes him, designating the place where the sofa should stand. Two other spots precede him, showing where the two chairs should stand. He puts the chairs there. (The spotlights are of different colours.) Another spot designates the place for the rocking chair. He follows it and places the rocking chair in its appointed spot. Another light already indicates the place for the little table. He puts it there. Another spot appears, designating the appropriate place for broom and shovel. He wants to put*

Sweep the floor in the direction of the boards.

When you clink glasses, they should ring clearly.

Every step must become completely natural to you.

You must be able to
act
independently.

Outside show is a poor substitute for
inner worth.

The merit of originality is not novelty; it is sincerity.

The golden rule in life is moderation in all things.

There's nothing in this world constant but inconstancy.

A bad beginning makes a bad ending.

Circumstances are beyond the control of man; but his conduct is in his own hands.

In an orderly room the soul also becomes orderly.

Every object you see for the second time you can already call your own.

The relativeness
of means
is your basic principle.

Running water

*them there but the spot moves on
and he follows it. It goes
backstage and he follows it there
with shovel and broom in hand.
The spot returns without him and
is already fixed on a place on the
stage when Kaspar returns. In
his arms he holds a large vase
with flowers. He puts the vase in
the designated place. Another
spot indicates a place on the little
table. Kaspar leaves the stage
and returns with a plateful of
decorative fruit. He puts it on
the little table. Another spot
designates an empty place in the
corner of the stage. He leaves the
stage and returns with a small
stool. He puts it in its appointed
place. Another spot indicates an
empty area on the backdrop. He
gives a sign to the stage-rigging
loft and a painting is lowered
on to the empty area. (What the
painting represents is of no
importance as long as it goes
with the furnishings.) Kaspar
directs it until it hangs perfectly.
He stands there. Another spot
walks ahead of him to the open
wardrobe. It lights up the clothes.
Kaspar goes to the wardrobe.
Quickly he takes off his jacket,
but finds no place to put it. The
spotlight goes backstage and he
follows it with the jacket over his
arm. He returns with a clothes
tree and hangs the jacket up on
it. He walks to the wardrobe and*

does not
become stagnant.

A room
should be
like a picture book.

Sitting all your life
is unhealthy.

A room
should have
a timeless character.

You must show
confidence
in your work.

There is no woodworm
in the door hinges.

You must be able to be proud
of what you have achieved.

Your well-being is determined
by your achievement.

The floor makes a decisive
difference in the overall
impression of the room.

What matters
is to be with it.

Doors lock, but also constitute
connections to the outside
world.

The objects
must supplement
your image.

All work is
what you
make of it.

*picks out another jacket, puts it
on, buttons it. He stands there.
He takes off his hat. He hangs
the hat up on the clothes tree.
The stage becomes increasingly
more colourful. He has now
begun to move in rhythm to the
sentences from the prompters. A
continuous sound has set in softly.
It now becomes louder. It is
apparent that the jacket goes
with the trousers and the other
objects. Everything on stage goes
with everything else. For a
moment Kaspar looks like a
dummy at an interior-decoration
exhibition. Only the open
wardrobe disrupts the harmony
of the picture. The continuous
tone becomes even louder. Kaspar
stands there and lets people look
him over. The stage is festively
lit.*

The order
should not be
a soul-less order.

You are
what you have.

Living in dark rooms
only makes for unnecessary
thoughts.

The order
of the objects
creates
all

prerequisites
for
happiness.

What is a nightmare in the dark
is
joyous certainty
in the light.

Every order
eventually looses its
terror.

You're not in the world for fun.

26
*The light on stage is very
gradually extinguished, the tone
adjusting itself to the light.
Kaspar is speaking as the light
goes out. He begins to speak in a
deep, well-modulated voice, but
raises it as the light and the
continuous sound subside. The
darker the stage and the softer*

*the tone, the more shrill and
ill-sounding Kaspar's voice
becomes. Finally, with the onset
of complete darkness and the
ceasing of the continuous sound,
he is whimpering in the highest
registers:* Everything that is
bright is peaceful: everything
that is quiet is peaceful:
everything that is in its place
is peaceful: everything peaceful
is friendly: everything friendly
is inhabitable: everything
inhabitable is comfortable:
everything comfortable is no
longer ominous: everything I
can name is no longer ominous:
everything that is no longer
ominous belongs to me: I am at
ease with everything that
belongs to me: everything I am
at ease with strengthens my
self-confidence: everything that
belongs to me is familiar to me:
everything I am familiar with
strengthens my self-confidence:
everything that is familiar to me
lets me breathe a sigh of relief:
everything I am familiar with is
orderly: everything that is
orderly is beautiful: everything
that is beautiful is good for my
eyes: everything that is good
for my eyes is good for me:
everything that is good for me
makes me good: everything
that makes me good makes me
good for something. *It is now
completely dark. As it again*

*The prompters speak while
Kaspar is speaking, however
without making him
incomprehensible, whereas they
themselves are only barely
comprehensible because they
speak too softly, their words
overlap, they leave out syllables,
reverse the order of the words, or
put the wrong emphasis on them.
In regular sequence they speak
something like the following text:*
Struck the table. Sat between
chairs. Rolled up the sleeves.
Stayed on the floor. Looked
behind curtains. Spat into
hands. Struck the table. Stayed
on the floor. Rolled up sleeves.
Sat down between chairs. Sat
down at the table together.
Struck the table. Sat down in
the nettles. Slammed the door.
Rolled up sleeves. Struck the
chairs. Beaten to a pulp. Struck
the table. Sat down in the
nettles. Knocked down. Spit in
front of feet. Struck between
the eyes. Broke the chain.
Stayed tough. Sat down in the
nettles. Knocked out. Beat
down the request. Showed the
fists. Beaten to a pulp. Struck
a low blow. Exterminated from

*becomes bright very gradually,
Kaspar begins to speak again, at
first with a pleasant-sounding
voice, but the brighter it becomes,
the higher and shriller his voice
gets :* Everything that is in order
is in order because I say to
myself that it is in order, just
as everything that lies on the
floor is a dead fly because I say
to myself that everything that
lies on the floor is only a dead
fly, just as everything that lies
on the floor lies there only for
a short while because I say to
myself that it lies there only for
a short while, just as everything
that lies gets up again because
I say to myself that it gets up
again, just as everything that I
say to myself is in order
because I say to myself that
everything that I say to myself
is in order.

head to toe. Smashed the floor.
Spat in front of the feet. Struck
between the eyes. Broke the
china. Pushed into the nettles.
Smashed the table. Struck a
low blow. Smashed the
communal table. Struck down.
Smashed the set. Smashed the
door. Struck down the heckler.
Stayed tough. Smashed all
prejudices.

### 27

*Kaspar is now taught the model
sentences with which an orderly
person struggles through life.
While he was uttering his last
sentences, he sat down in the
rocking chair. During the
following course of instruction he
continues to sit in the chair, but
begins to rock only gradually. At
first he drawls his words,
although speaking with intensity,
without punctuation marks; then*

*While Kaspar is sitting in the
rocking chair, the words the
prompters uttered just now,
which anticipate the aphorisms,
are repeated : now, because
Kaspar is silent, they are more
comprehensible and become
completely comprehensible
towards the end, and then turn
into the following model
sentences :* Every sentence helps
you along: you get over every

*he begins to speak with full stops, finally with hyphens, finally he makes exaggerated sense, and ultimately he utters model sentences.*

object with a sentence: a sentence helps you get over an object when you can't really get over it, so that you really get over it: a sentence helps you to get over every other sentence by letting itself take the place of the other sentence: the door has two sides: truth has two sides: if the door had three sides, truth would have three sides: the door has many sides: truth has many sides: the door: the truth: no truth without a door. You beat the dust off your trousers: you beat the thought out of your head: if you couldn't beat the dust off your trousers, you couldn't beat the thought out of your head. You finish speaking: you finish thinking: if you couldn't finish speaking, you couldn't say the sentence: I finish thinking. You look again: you think again: if you couldn't look again, you couldn't say the sentence: I think again: if you couldn't look again, you couldn't think again.

The pupil of the eye is round fear is round had the pupil perished fear would have perished but the pupil is there and fear is there if the pupil weren't honest I couldn't say fear is honest if the pupil were not permitted fear wouldn't be

permitted no fear without pupil
if the pupil weren't moderate
I couldn't say fear only arises
at room temperature fear is less
honest than is permitted fear is
drenched warm as a hand on
the contrary

You are standing. The table is
standing. The table is not
standing, it was placed there.
You are lying. The corpse is
lying. The corpse is not lying,
it was placed there. If you
couldn't stand and if you
couldn't lie, you couldn't say:
the table is standing, and the
corpse is lying: if you couldn't
lie and stand, you couldn't
say: I can neither lie nor stand.

A fat man is true to life cold
sweat is commonplace if a fat
man weren't true to life and if
his cold sweat weren't
commonplace a fat man
couldn't become afraid and if a
fat man couldn't lie on his
stomach I couldn't say he
neither stands up nor can he
sing

The room is small but mine.
The stool is low but
comfortable. The sentence is
harsh but just. The rich man is
rich but friendly. The poor man
is poor but happy. The old man
is old but sturdy. The star is

famous but modest. The madman is mad but harmless. The criminal is scum but a human being none the less. The cripple is pitiable but also a human being. The stranger is different, but it doesn't matter:

But the snow falls contentedly. The fly runs over the water but not excessively. The soldier crawls through the mud but pleasurably. The whip cracks on the back but aware of its limits. The fool runs into the trap but at peace with the world. The condemned man leaps into the air but judiciously. The factory gate squeaks but that passes away.

The ring is decorative as well as an object of value. The community is not only a burden but also a joy. War is indeed a misfortune, but sometimes inescapable. The future is obscure but it also belongs to the enterprising. Playing is not only a diversion, but is also a preparation for reality. Force is indeed a dubious method, but it can be useful. A harsh youth is indeed unjust, but it makes you hard. Hunger is bad indeed, but there are worse things. Whipping is reprehensible indeed, but one also has to see the positive side:

47

The sunflowers are not only abundant, but also summer and winter. The corners are glowing indeed, but for dying of thirst they are not only made to order but also spend a meditative old age observed by daylight. The better solutions are not only not worth striving for, but indeed eat right out of my hand, yet will also decisively and emphatically reject any and all interference.

The more lovingly the table has been laid, the more you love to come home. The greater the want of space, the more dangerous the thoughts. The more happily you work, the more quickly you find a way to yourself. The more self-assured you are, the easier it is for you to get ahead. The greater the mutual trust, the more bearable the living together. The more the hand perspires, the less sure of himself the man is. The cleaner the flat, the cleaner the tenant. The farther south you go, the lazier the people:

The more wood on the roof, the more mildew in the bread oven. The more cities with cellars, the more machinations on the slag heaps. The brighter the clotheslines, the more suicides in the trade department. The more emphatic the demand for reason in the mountains, the more ingratiating the dog-eat-dog laws of free nature.

It goes without saying that a large vase stands on the floor, just as it goes without saying that a smaller vase stands on a stool, while it goes without saying that an even smaller vase stands on a chair, just as it goes without saying that an even smaller vase stands on the table, while it goes without saying that creepers stand even higher. It goes without saying that well-being is determined by achievement. It goes without saying that despair is out of place here:

It goes without saying that the flour sack strikes the rat dead. It goes without saying that hot bread lets children come prematurely into the world. It goes without saying that discarded matches introduce a demonstration of confidence.

You gain something new from each object. No one stands on the sidelines. Every day the sun rises. No one is irreplaceable. Every new building means peace. No one is an island. Every industrious person is liked everywhere. No one is

Every split straw is a vote for the progressive forces. No country fair means security for all. Each dripping tap is an example of a healthy life. No sensible arm is lifted for the burning department store. Every pneumatic-drill operator who comes upon a corpse corresponds to a rapid-firing mechanism that can deliver six thousand rounds per minute.

A cat is no getting on. A stone is not a completely satisfied need. A straw man is no body count. Running away is no equality of rights. To stretch a rope across the path is no permanent value.

allowed to shirk his task. Each new shoe hurts in the beginning. No one has the right to exploit another. Every courteous person is punctual. No one who has a high opinion of himself lets others do his work for him. Every sensible person will bear the whole situation in mind with every step he takes. No one points the finger at others. Every person deserves respect, even a cleaning woman.

Poverty is no disgrace. War is not a game. A state is not a gangster organization. A flat is no sanctuary. Work is no picnic. Freedom is no licence. Silence is no excuse. A conversation is no interrogation.

The appendix bursts. The grenade bursts. If the appendix couldn't burst, you couldn't say: the grenade bursts.

The dog barks. The commander barks.

The water is rising. The fever is rising. If the water couldn't rise, the fever couldn't rise.

The avalanche roars. The angry man roars.

The angry man thunders. Thunder thunders. Without the angry man, thunder couldn't thunder.

The flags flutter. The eyelids flutter.

The balloon swells. The jubilation swells. Without the balloon, the jubilation couldn't swell.

The laughing man gurgles. The swamp gurgles.

The nervous nelly jerks. The hanged man jerks. If it weren't for the nervous nelly, the hanged man couldn't jerk.

The firewood cracks. The bones crack.

The blood screams to high heaven. The injustice screams to high heaven. Without the blood, injustice could not scream to high heaven.

The door springs open. The skin springs open. The match burns. The slap burns. The grass trembles. The fearful girl trembles. The slap in the face

smacks. The body smacks. The
tongue licks. The flame licks.
The saw screeches. The torture
victim screeches. The lark trills.
The policeman trills. The
blood stops. The breath stops.

It is not true that the conditions
are as they are represented; on
the contrary, it is true that the
conditions are different from
their representation.

It is untrue that the
representation of the
conditions is the only possible
representation of the conditions:
on the contrary, it is true that
there exist other possibilities of
the representation of the
conditions. *Kaspar speaks along
with the prompters to the end of
this sequence.*

It is untrue that the
representation of the conditions
is the only possible
representation of the conditions:
on the contrary, it is true that
there exist other possibilities of
the representation of the
conditions. It does not
correspond to the facts to
represent the conditions at all;
on the contrary, it corresponds
to the facts not to represent
them at all. That the
conditions correspond to the
facts is untrue.

You bend down; someone sees
you, you rise; you see yourself.
You move yourself; someone
reminds you; you set yourself
down; you remember yourself.
You are afraid of yourself;
someone quiets you; someone
explains you; you rush
yourself; you explain yourself;
you disquiet yourself:

I am quieting myself.

You were already making a fist.

I was still screaming.

You still took a deep breath.

I was already there.

The chair still stands in its place.

I was still standing.

Nothing has changed yet.

I was already awake.

The door is already shut tight.

I was already kicking.

Some were still sleeping.

I am whispering already.

One can still hear knocking on the wall.

I still wasn't hearing anything.

Some never learn.

I am outside already.

Here and there someone is still moving.

I still don't believe it.

Many are already placing their hands on the head.

I am already running.

Some are still breathing.

I am pulling in my head already.

Someone still objected.

I am already hearing.

A single person is still
whispering.

I already understand.

Single shots are still being fired.

I know already.

you

passed

you

living weight

you

light and easy

you

within reach

you

nothing to look for

you

a better life

you

good laugh

you

master everything

you

will win everywhere

you

lowered the mother mortality

                              you

was leading

                              you

more and more comprehensively

                              you

free of

                              you

is peace and future

                              you

a relationship to the world

                              you

which moved things closer

                              you

peaceful purposes

                              you

constant growing

                              you

in case of emergency to

                              you

only for protection

                              you

irresistibly

                              you

reached

                              you

55

trampled

               you

called

               you

was and is

               you

recognized myself.

You know what you are saying.
You say what you are thinking.
You think like you feel. You
feel what it depends on.

You know on what it depends.
You know what you want. You
can if you want to. You can if
you only want to. You can if
you must.

You only want what everyone
wants. You want because you
feel pressed. You feel you can
do it. You must because you
can.

Say what you think. You can't
say except what you think. You
can't say anything except what
you are also thinking. Say what
you think. When you want to
say what you don't think you
must begin to think it that very
moment. Say what you think.
You can begin to speak. You
must begin to speak. When you
begin to speak you will begin
to think what you speak even

when you want to think something different. Say what you think. Say what you don't think. When you have begun to speak you will think what you are saying. You think what you are saying, that means you can think what you are saying, that means it is good that you think what you are saying, that means you ought to think what you are saying, that means, on the one hand, that you may think what you are saying, and on the other hand, that you must think what you are saying, because you are not allowed to think anything *different* from what you are saying. Think what you are saying:

When I am, I was. When I was, I am. When I am, I will be. When I will be, I was. Although I was, I will be. Although I will be, I am. As often as I am, I have been. As often as I have been, I was. While I was, I have been. While I have been, I will be. Since I will be, I will have been. Since I have been, I am. Due to the fact that I am, I have been. Due to the fact that I have been, I was. Without having been, I was. Without having been, I will be. So that I will be, I have been. So that I will have been, I have been.

Before I was, I was. Before I
had become, I am. I am so that
I will have become. I will have
become so that I was. I was as
soon as I will have become. I
will have become as soon as I
will be. I will be while I will
have become. I will have
become while I had become. I
became because I will have
become. I will have become
because I became. I became
because I will have become. I
will have become because I am.
I am the one I am.
I am the one I am.
I am the one I am.

*Kaspar stops rocking.*

Why are there so many black
worms flying about?

*The stage becomes black.*

28

*As it grows light again after
several moments of quiet, the
prompters speak once more :* You
have model sentences with
which you can get through life:
by applying these models to
your sentences, you can impose
order on everything that
appears disorderly: you can
declare it ordered: every object
can be what you designate it to
be: if you *see* the object
differently from the way you

*speak* of it, you must be
mistaken: you must say to
yourself that you are mistaken
and you *will* see the object: if
you don't *want* to say that to
yourself, then it is obvious that
you want to be forced, and
really want to say it after all.

*It has now become very bright.
Kaspar is quiet.*

29

You can learn and make
yourself useful. Even if there
are no limits: you can draw
them. You can perceive: notice:
become aware in all innocence:
every object becomes a
valuable. You can develop in
an orderly fashion.

*It becomes even brighter. Kaspar
is even quieter.*

30

You can quiet yourself with
sentences: you can be nice and
quiet.

*It is very bright. Kaspar is very
quiet.*

31

You've been cracked open.

*The stage becomes dark suddenly.*
*After a moment :* You become
sensitive to dirt.

*It becomes bright, but not very.*
*Kaspar is sitting in the rocking*
*chair. A second Kaspar with the*
*same kind of face-like mask, the*
*same costume, comes on stage*
*from the wings. He enters,*
*sweeping with a broom. He*
*quickly cleans the stage, each*
*movement being made distinctly*
*visible, for example, by the spot.*
*In passing he gives the wardrobe*
*door a shove, but it won't stay*
*shut. He cleans carefully under*
*the sofa. He sweeps the dirt into*
*a pile at the edge on the side of*
*the stage. He walks across the*
*stage to fetch the shovel. He*
*walks back to the pile of dirt and*
*sweeps the dirt on to the shovel.*
*He does not succeed in sweeping*
*the dirt on to the shovel with a*
*single swipe of the broom, nor*
*quite with the second swipe. By*
*zigzagging backwards across the*
*stage, between objects, without*
*however bothering the first*
*Kaspar, he continues to try to*
*sweep the rest of the dirt on to the*
*shovel. He sweeps and sweeps*
*until he disappears backstage. At*
*that moment the stage darkens.*

34

*After a moment :* Become aware
that you are moving.

35
*It becomes bright. A third
Kaspar appears on stage from
the wings, accompanying a fourth
Kaspar, who walks on crutches,
dragging his legs, moving very
very slowly, almost imperceptibly.
The third Kaspar repeatedly
increases his pace somewhat, but
each time has to wait for the
fourth Kaspar to catch up with
him. That takes time. They walk
across stage front, Kaspar 3
nearer to the audience than
Kaspar 4. Kaspar 3 to some
extent adopts the gait of Kaspar
4, but in part retains his own
manner of walking and therefore
still has to wait for Kaspar 4 to
catch up with him. So both are
lurching, as they say, almost
'unbearably' slowly across the
stage, past Kaspar 1. When they
have finally gone, the stage
darkens instantly.*

36

*After a moment :* What you
can't handle, you can play with.

## 37

*It becomes bright. Two further Kaspars come towards each other across the stage from different directions. They want to get past each other. Both step aside in the same direction, and bump into each other. They step aside in the other direction, and bump into each other again. They repeat the attempt in the first direction, and almost bump into each other. What looked awkward and unnatural at first gradually assumes a rhythm. The movements become more rapid and also more regular. The two Kaspars no longer walk into each other. Finally they move only the upper part of their body, then only their heads jerk, and finally they stand still. The next moment they make a wide, elegant curve around each other and walk off stage to the left and right. During these attempts at circumnavigation, Kaspar 1 has tried to fold an unfolded road map. He does not succeed. Finally he begins playing with the map, as though it were an accordion, say. Suddenly the map lets itself be folded thus, and that is the moment when the other Kaspars leave the stage and it darkens.*

38

*After a moment:* To become
aware that everything falls back
into order of its own accord.

39
*It becomes bright. Another
Kaspar steps out of the wings. He
steps in front of the sofa, on
which there is a thick cushion.
He pushes with one fist into the
cushion and steps aside. The
audience sees the cushion slowly
regain its original shape. This
can also be projected on the
backdrop. With a final tiny jolt,
the cushion regains its original
form. The stage darkens at once.*

40

*After a moment:* Movements.

41
*Another Kaspar steps on stage.
He has a ball in one hand. He
places the ball on the floor and
steps back. The ball rolls off.
Kaspar 1 puts the ball where it
was first. The ball rolls off.
Kaspar holds his hand on the
ball for a considerable period of
time. He steps back. The ball
rolls off. The stage darkens.*

*After a moment :* Pains.

*It is still dark; the audience sees
two matches being lit on stage.
When it grows bright again,
Kaspar 1 is sitting in the rocking
chair, the other Kaspar on the
sofa. Each is holding a burning
match between his fingers. The
flames touch the fingers. Neither
Kaspar emits a sound. The stage
darkens.*

*After a moment :* Sounds.

*As it becomes bright, Kaspar 1 is
alone on stage, standing by the
large table. He takes the
broad-necked bottle and pours a
little water into the glass standing
next to the bottle. The sound of
pouring water is distinctly
audible. He stops pouring.
Quickly he pours the water from
the glass back into the bottle. He
takes the bottle and pours water
slowly into the glass. The sound
of pouring water is even more
distinct. When the glass is full,
the stage darkens.*

46

*After a moment :* A tone.

47
*When it becomes bright, even
more quickly than before, another
Kaspar is standing at the side of
the stage while Kaspar 1 is
standing by the table. He is
holding a thick roll of paper
which is held together by a
rubber band. Slowly but surely
he forces the rubber band off the
roll. The band snaps off, a tone
is heard. At once the stage
darkens.*

48

*After a moment :* A view.

49
*The audience hears a noise while
the stage is still dark. When it
becomes bright, Kaspar 1 is again
alone on the stage, sitting by the
table with the plastic fruit on it.
He is holding a partially peeled
apple in his hand. He continues
peeling, the peel growing longer
and longer, and stops peeling
shortly before the apple has been
completely peeled. He places the
apple on top of the decorative
fruit. The peel hangs way down.
The stage darkens.*

*The prompters remain silent.*

*It becomes bright. Kaspar is standing in the centre of the stage, between the table and the wardrobe. With one hand he is forcibly opening the other hand, which is a fist, finger by finger. The fist resists more and more tenaciously. Finally he wrenches open the hand. It is empty. The stage darkens.*

52

*It quickly becomes bright. Another Kaspar is sitting on the sofa. Kaspar sees the other Kaspar. The stage darkens.*

53

*It becomes bright even more quickly. Kaspar is again alone on the stage, standing in front of the wardrobe, his face to the audience. The stage darkens.*

54

*It becomes bright more quickly still. Kaspar looks down at himself. The stage darkens.*

55

*Kaspar tries to catch himself. First he runs in a wide circle across the stage, then in smaller circles, spiralling in on himself until he turns on the same spot. He reaches for himself but, because he is standing on one spot, only seizes himself with his own arms . . . whereupon he becomes still and the stage darkens.*

**56**
*It becomes bright more quickly still. Kaspar is standing in front of the wardrobe, his back to the audience. It darkens.*


**57**
*It becomes bright. Kaspar is in the process of closing the wardrobe doors. He presses on them for some time. He steps back. The doors stay shut. The stage darkens.*


**58**
*It becomes bright. It is very bright. Kaspar leans back against the wardrobe. The stage looks harmonious. A chord. A spotlight is trained on Kaspar. He assumes various poses. He continues to alter the position of his arms and legs. Say, his arms are akimbo, he shoves one leg forward, lets his arms drop, crosses his legs, puts his hands in his pockets, first in his trouser pockets, then in his jacket pockets, stands there with his legs apart, finally crosses his hands over his stomach, puts his feet close together, finally his arms are akimbo again. His legs are still close together. He begins to speak:*

I am healthy and strong. I am honest and frugal. I am conscientious. I am industrious, reticent and modest. I am always friendly. I make no great demands. My ways are winning and natural. Everyone likes me. I can deal with everything. I am here for everyone. My love of order and cleanliness has never given reason for complaint. My knowledge is above average. Everything I am asked to do, I do perfectly. Anyone can provide the desired information about me. I am peace-loving and have an untarnished record. I am not one of those who start a big hue and cry over every little thing. I am calm, dutiful, and receptive. I can become enthusiastic about every worthy cause. I would like to get ahead. I would like to learn. I would like to be useful. I have a concept of length, height, and breadth. I know what matters. I treat objects with feeling. I have already become used to everything. I am better. I am well. I am ready to die. My head feels light. I can finally be left alone. I would like to put my best foot forward. I don't accuse anyone. I laugh a lot. I can make heads and tails of everything. I have no unusual characteristics. I don't show my upper gums when I laugh. I have no scar under the right eye and no birthmark under the left ear. I am no public menace. I would like to be a member. I would like to cooperate. I am proud of what has been achieved so far. I am taken care of for the moment. I am prepared to be interrogated. A new part of my life lies ahead of me. That is my right hand, that is my left hand. If worst comes to worst, I can hide under the furniture. It was always my wish to be with it.

*He pulls away from the wardrobe, takes two or three steps, the wardrobe stays shut:*

Once I felt as though I didn't even exist; now I exist almost too much, and the objects, of which there were too many at one time, now have become almost too few.

*In the meantime he has walked farther forward. The wardrobe stays shut:*

Once plagued by sentences
I now can't have enough of sentences.
Once haunted by words
I now play with every single letter.

*He remains standing in the same spot:*

At one time I only spoke when asked,
now I speak of my own accord, but now
I can wait to speak until I am asked.

*He takes one or two steps more:*

Earlier on, each rational sentence was a burden to me
and I detested each rational order
but from now on
I will be rational.

*He either does or does not take a step:*

Earlier, I threw down one chair, then a second, and then a third:
now, with the introduction of order, my habits are changing.

*He takes roughly one step:*

I am quiet
now I do not want
to be someone else any more
nothing incites me
against myself any more.
Every object
has become

accessible
to me
and I
am receptive
to each object.
Now I know what I want:
I want
to be
quiet
and every object
that I find ominous
I designate as mine
so that it stops
being sinister to me.

*He walks off to the side of the stage but returns after several steps, as though he still had something more to say. He says nothing. He leaves again, taking more steps than the last time, but again steps half-way back on to the stage, as though he had something left to say. He says nothing. He almost leaves, but takes one or two steps back, again as though he had something left to say. He says nothing. Then he departs rapidly. On the now uninhabited stage the wardrobe doors gradually open. When the wide-open wardrobe doors have come to a complete rest, the stage darkens at a stroke, at the same time the auditorium becomes bright. It is intermission. The auditorium doors are opened.*


59
*After a few moments the INTERMISSION TEXT is piped through loud-speakers into the auditorium, into the lobbies, and even out on to the street if that is possible. At first these texts are quite low and barely audible. The texts consist of tapes of the prompters' speeches, sheer noise, actual taped speeches by party leaders, popes, public speakers of every kind, presidents and prime ministers, perhaps even statements by writers and poets speaking at official functions. The sentences should never be complete, but should be complemented and superseded by other mangled sentences. Although the audience should not be kept from entering into well-deserved conversation, its relaxed mood ought to be disturbed now and then by the intermission texts. Some members of the audience might even be able to listen with one ear while devoting themselves to their*

*drinks. The text might be as follows: (Noises, such as the clinking of glasses.)* free of all worries of the present, we will have the last word. The surplus is lower than the criterion which has been anticipated. *(Louder clinking of glasses.)* What once was not an incalculable demand now becomes much too unexpected for many, and much too early. We need more courage if we can't be saved. A new mass flight south is more important than a murder that never occurred. It is often unjustly forgotten how healthy it is to be a Marine. We want to work to the last man. Don't think of what your country can do for you but climb up the wall. *(The sound of a large truck approaching, then disappearing.)* Criticism helps all real progress no matter the deposits in the glands. Animal herds should beware of the clear mountain air. The results exist to be burned without compunction. Without a certain number of dead each week, it neither goes upward nor downward. Hunger helps no one and doesn't teach anyone manners. *(Meanwhile, the blades of a large rotary saw have begun to clatter. This sound becomes increasingly loud.)* In recent times the voices have increased that have great difficulty playing with themselves. The sides of the scale of justice lower themselves towards each other at the end although everyone is prepared to make sacrifices. With respect to the rat plague we must reach a mutually satisfactory result. Everyone should finally open his ears and listen to the truth when the brand name is announced. What now matters most is to objectively examine the whole realm of concepts associated with each demand. No one can depend on the fact that dooms the situation. *(The saw blades penetrate wood with a screech; however, the noise soon turns into that of a gentle waterfall.)* Nothing that comes from the outside is a distorted picture simply for that and no other simple reason. The human element appears quite ineradicable. We always exist under the condition that we refuse to let irresponsible circles rob us of the view of the public nuisance which is the world. Every declaration of war is designed for each case of patience which has been exhausted. Convincing someone in the nicest possible manner does not have to end with a blow of the water level on the head. Everyone is called upon to the extent of calling the thing by its well-deserved name. The police always has a time of it because it must justify itself. None of us is entirely innocent of the time of day. *(Whistling, booing, stomping, the sound of waves.)* A sceptical stock market gets off best. At least we don't want the employees to have to pay extra even though many things speak for breaking it off. Impudence itself is no silver star. Of course the refugees have to be helped but running away with bare feet is not one of our problems. We know how to handle the glasses more and more. Uniformed persons know the difficulties when it suddenly becomes dark. The robes of the judges are breathtaking when all that is at stake is the shabby whole. We all want to move with profound seriousness which is what matters. (*A swelling football cheer which breaks off with a profound sigh, then a resurgence of it which turns into regularly increasing and decreasing cheers.*) Gripping is easier than finding oneself a well-deserved flat. We'll inflict injuries on the head and chest of anyone who is of the same opinion as we are. The right of hospitality not only cannot be superseded as a concept but one must point to it if necessary with a brain stroke. A screwdriver in the windpipe is appropriate remuneration for someone who never did anything but someone else's duty. Anyone who considers himself someone loses his nerve when angling. We'll accept anyone into the bargain who shakes the foundations. (*A sharply braking car; simultaneously, a jet of water from a firehose.*) The transformation of society into any number of possible mass demonstrations corresponds to a pacifier for a blind man. The war in the sandbox has cost many a live corpse. Anyone who thinks the way he acts only strengthens the neck of the one who thinks differently. No one deserves a fate that makes him level with the ground. Life used to be more worth while at one time but now it is no brushfire any more. (*Long-drawn-out factory siren or foghorn.*) What was said of the property owners matters even less with respect to the flesh wounds. Anyone who kills in blind fury fools himself to an extent that is questionable in the least. Anyone who protests against the delivery of goods must also protest against revisionist thinking. We value the strength of a freely reached decision more than sharks chasing swimmers. Self-assurance contributes a great deal towards continuing useful conversations. Too little has been said so far about the minorities who proudly crawl off into their corners. (*The scraping of chairs on a stone floor.*) What was once forbidden has now been outlawed. Every outward order enables a peaceful and measured exchange of ideas. We regard the either/or as the mark of a free man. We all have to make an effort to be understanding when a dead man assumes the colour of grass. A murder does not necessarily have to be equated with a nose dive. A third-degree burn clogs every petrol line. (*Sounds of horses' hoofs, together with the sound of seats being turned up, street noises, doors being slammed shut, typewriter noises.*) No one is beaten until he is ripe for retirement without good reason. The right to own estates requires no elaborate justification. A loosening-up exercise corresponds to the length of a truncheon between two legs. Whereas every suicide used to be left-handed, the regulation has now become uniform. No lull in the fighting permits time to count the sleeping flies on the ceiling of the cowshed. A single person perched on the church steeple can be equated with an incitement to riot. If one confronts a violent person by oneself, one is oneself a violent person, whereas when one confronts a violent person in the company of six or four men, thereupon the former becomes gentle of his own accord and is gentle. (*Even before this last sentence, the sounds have changed and become distorted musical noises, as if a record is being played at inordinately slow speed; a monotonous, rhythmic music should be utilized for this purpose. In between a tap is gradually turned on to full strength, then the plug in a bathtub is pulled out; in addition there may be heavy breathing noises, then the sound of whiplashes, sudden bursts of laughter as after a joke, women's laughter as if at a cocktail party. While all this is going on, the audience should be able to hear, although not quite comprehending, the spoken text. Then follows a short moment of quiet, then noise once again and the reading of texts, then a longer moment of quiet, then something like the following text by itself.*) A beautifully laid table. Everything in the best order. You're in no great hurry. You help your companion take off the coat. The colourful tablecloth delights everyone. The knife lies on the right. The napkin on the left. The plate stands in the middle. The cup stands at the right and to the back. The knife lies in front of the cup. The towel hangs to the right of the knife. Your finger rests on the towel. To the right of the towel is the first-aid kit. The plates are handed from the left. The soup is handed from the right. The drinks are handed from the right. Everything that you serve yourself is handed from the left. The stab comes from the right. You are sitting in the middle. The salt cellar stands on the left. The spoon is lying on the outside to the right of the knife. The spoon lies bottom up. The grip that chokes comes from both sides. Your hand is lying on the table. The edge of the knife is facing left. As seen from your seat, the heart of the person opposite you is on the right. The glass stands to the right of the plate. You drink in small sips. The blow is more effective when it comes from below. The bouquet of flowers is in the centre of the table. The fork lies to the left of the plate. You can't give white flowers to the dying. You sit upright on principle. The older one is on the right. The bouquet does not block your view of the person opposite you. The biscuit plate is in the middle of each setting. The coal pile is under the table. You are not resting your head on your arms. You always look for friendly words. The victim of an assassination lies in the middle of each setting. The candelabra stand in the centre of the table. A spot on a shirt is an everyday occurrence. It is not unusual for the knife to slip on the plate. Your neighbour's hand is resting on the knife. You do not swallow the wrong way. You converse to your left and to your right. (*Again the inordinately slow music has come on with a crash that is not recognizable as music at first. Houses crumble, bombs crash, but at a great distance; the text is gradually made unintelligible by the noises and finally is entirely suppressed; in between the audience begins to hear the bell as well as taped chimes; rattling, gongs, factory sirens as well as the theatre bell that calls the audience back to the auditorium.*)

60
*While the lights in the auditorium are slowly dimmed in a theatrical manner, the open stage is only moderately lighted. The objects are in exactly the same position as before the intermission. The wardrobe is open. Two Kaspars are sitting on the sofa, close together. They are silent. The masks now evince an expression of contentment. After a few moments of silence, the prompters begin to recite all over the room:*

61

> While giving a thrashing
> you are never as calm
> as when beating
> a rug
> Intermittent smashing
> of a stick
> on your jug
> is no balm
> nor a reason

to bewail the lack of law and
order
this season
a sip of lye
in your mug
or a prick
in the guts
or a stick
in the nuts
being wriggled about
or something on that order
only pricklier
fearlessly
introduced in the ears
so
as to
get someone hopping
and pop in order
by all means
at your command
but chiefly
without being
overly
fussy
over the means –
that
is no reason
to lose any words
over the lack of order:
for
while you are popping other
to put them in order
for better or worse
you force them to sing
whereas –
once they are
completely in order
and those who were fooling
around

have been made to look
foolish –
you can sing
yourself
and after the thrashing –
when your fists and feet
are idle –
you can beat the rug
to calm yourself down.

*A third Kaspar with a small
package wrapped in wrapping
paper comes out of the wings and
sits down next to the other two
Kaspars, sits down in an orderly
fashion, the package on his knees.*

While putting other in order
you are not as quiet and orderly
as later on
when you –
having been put in order
yourself by the thrashing
that you've given others –
want to enjoy
a well-ordered
world
and can enjoy
such a world
with an untroubled
conscience.

*A fourth Kaspar comes on stage
with a similar package. Kaspar 3
makes room for him between
himself and the other two
Kaspars. Kaspar 4 sits down
quietly. All four Kaspars are
still.*

While giving
a thrashing
it would be foolish
to think of the future
but in the pauses
between punches
it's delicious
to imagine the time
of imminent order –
so that a kick
that is a touch too disorderly
won't contribute
when the thrashing
resumes
to channelling
the thoughts
of the socially sick
– when he's adjusting
later on –
in the wrong direction.

*A fifth Kaspar enters with a
similar but perhaps larger
package. Kaspar 3 gets up.
Kaspar 5 takes Kaspar 3's place.
Kaspar 3 squeezes himself into
the small space left next to
Kaspar 4. Kaspar 5 puts the
package in front of him on the
floor. All five are still.*

But should an inordinate
beating of the heart fail to
occur
while you are thrashing away
and your fists
beat the breath
from the victim's lung
like (to use the same image

again)
dust
from a rug
and you straighten out
the wretch's tongue
(to use the same image again)
like fringes on a rug
only then does the injustice
occur:
for
while you are thrashing away
you can't be as easy
as when beating a rug
while plugging up a mouth
you must be un-
easy:
so as not to become un-
easy
later on:
the failure of an inordinate
beating of the beater's hearth
to occur while he is giving a
thrashing
is BAD!
for
anyone whose hand has
suitably trembled while giving
a thrashing
has clean hands
and is just one more person
who'll have to have no qualms
later on:
thus calm reigns on earth.

*The original Kaspar comes on
stage as he did at first, but
without having to look for the
slit in the curtain. His movements
are self-assured and he looks like*

*the other Kaspars. His mask too*
*should show a contented*
*expression. He walks with firm*
*steps to the front of the stage, as*
*though to take a bow, nicely*
*avoiding all objects. He stops in*
*front of the microphone. All six*
*Kaspars are still.*

Those
who have been put in order –
instead of retreating
into themselves
or fleeing
society –
should now make a real effort
without being compelled to or
thrashed
but out of their own free will
to show new paths
by looking for sentences
that are valid for all:
it is not so much that they *can*
choose
but that they *must* choose
and tell the others –
without empty sayings
or blown-up phrases –
the unadorned truth
about themselves:
and the others too
should finally be able to want
to do
what they themselves
want, ought and can do.

62
*Kaspar, at the microphone,*
*begins to speak. His voice begins*

*to resemble the voices of the*
*prompters.*
Although
long in the world
I grasped
nothing
I asked
about the ob-
vious
and found
every-
thing
fi-
nite
and infi-
nite
ridi-
culous
every object
appalled me
and the whole world
galled me
neither
did I want to be
myself
nor did I want to be
somebody else
my own
hand
was unknown
to me
my own
legs
walked
of their own
accord
I was
in a deep
sleep

with open
eyes:
I was unconscious
as though
drunk
and though
I was
supposed to be of use
I was
of no use
each sight
produced dislike
in me
each sound
deceived me
about itself
each new step
caused nausea and sucking
in my chest
I couldn't keep up
I blocked my sight
myself
no light
lit up
for me
with the whole mish-
mash
of sentences
I never hit
on the idea
that it
was meant
for me
I noticed nothing
of what was happening
around me
before I began getting
on to the world.

I felt
the caco-
pho-
ny
and screa-
ming
as
a roa-
ring
and gurg-
ling
in my guts
I couldn't keep one thing apart
from another
three
was not
more than two
and when I was in the sun
it rained
and when I sweated
in the sun
or was getting warm
during a run
I fended off the sweat
with an umbrella
I could keep nothing apart
neither hot
from cold
nor black
from white
neither old
from new
nor day
from night
neither people

from objects
nor prayer
from blasphemy
each room
looked flat
to me
and scarcely
was I awake
when the flat
objects
fell
all over me
as in a night-
mare:
they resisted
me
everything unknown
interrogated
me
simultaneously
everything I couldn't keep apart
confused me
and drove me
wild
so that I became lost
among the objects
and to find my way out
destroyed them.

*He is quiet for a few moments.*
*The Kaspars behind him are*
*quiet too.*

I got
on to the world
not
by the clock
it was the pain
when I fell

which helped me
drive
a wedge
between me
and the objects
and finally
rid me
of my babbling:
thus the pain
drove the confusion
out of me.

I learned
to fill
the void
with words
I learned
who
was
who
and to still
everything shrill
with sentences
no empty bed
confused my head
any more
everything
is at my will
never
again
will
I shudder
before an empty wardrobe
before empty
boxes
empty
rooms
I hesitate
before no walk

out
into the open
for every crack
in the wall
I have wiles
that help me keep
the situation well
under control.

*He now raises his tone. The light
becomes brighter. The other
Kaspars are still silent.*

Everyone must be free
everyone must be able to see
everyone must know what he
wants
no one should be bothered by
anyone's taunts
no one may miss
the drill
no one may kill
himself or anyone else
everyone must live his own life
no one may beat his wife
everyone must give his best
everyone must pass the test
no one may miss
the boat
no one may piss
on those below
everyone must look
everyone in the eye
everyone must feel loose
everyone must cook
his own goose
everyone must give
everyone what is his.

*The other Kaspars on the sofa
begin to emit peculiar noises
whose significance is unmistakable.
The audience hears suggestions of
stylized sobbing, imitation wind
sounds, giggling.*

Everyone must be his own man
everyone must know the lay of
the land
everyone must watch what
everyone says
no one may blindly trust
another man's gaze
everyone must see the other's
good side too
no one may willy nilly sail out
into the blue
everyone must let himself be
led
no one may let
lies to be spread
about anyone.

*To some extent simultaneously
with Kaspar's speaking, the
audience hears grumbling,
croaking, lamenting, falsetto
singing, owl-like hooting coming
from behind him.*

Everyone must work
on himself
Everyone must shirk
from quarrelling with others
everyone must also care for the
other
everyone must think of the
future

everyone must feel completely
secure.

*The audience hears rustling,*
*leaves slapping against each*
*other, ululations, roaring,*
*laughter, humming, purring,*
*warbling, and a single sharp*
*scream.*

Everyone must wash his hands
before eating
everyone must take off his
trousers
before a beating
no one may eat
out of anyone's hands
everyone must treat
the other
like a brother
everyone must be neat-
ly combed for the meal
says mother
no one may let the other
whimper and wail
everyone must cut his
fingernails
everyone must lend a hand
no one may spoil
the land
no one may soil
the clean doilies
everyone must clean
his nose
everyone should smell like a
rose
no one may make fun of other
blokes
with foolish jokes

86

no one may tickle
anyone
during the burial
no one may scribble
on toilet walls
no one may rend
the law books
everyone must lend
everyone an ear
no one is allowed to fear
everyone must tell everyone his
name.

*In the meantime, the noises and
sounds in the background have
risen to such an extent that
Kaspar in front must raise his
voice more and more. At the end
of his rhymes, the other Kaspars
are still sitting quietly on the
sofa – trilling, twittering, clearing
their throats, groaning, heckling,
etc. But these sounds have let
Kaspar's speech become so loud
that the last words resemble the
thunderous ending of a speech.*

63
*The Kaspars in back are quiet
for the moment. Kaspar in front
begins to sing, perhaps falsetto.
Slowly but surely the prompters
chime in, in canon fashion,
which, however, is not resolved.
They sing softly and delicately,
so that Kaspar is intelligible
throughout. Kaspar sings like a
true believer.*

No one may bite
the fork with his teeth
no one may cite
the names of murderers at
dinner
no one may grease
the palm of a sinner
no one may transport private
persons

in the official car
no one may start a fight
in a bar
every one must be worth
everyone's while
no one may be vile
to a woman who's giving birth
no one may call a man
by another man's
name
no one may ridicule
anyone
just because he has thick lips
no one may stick a knife
between anyone's ribs
everyone must call a cop on the
street
officer sir

*The Kaspars behind him also sing*
*along, but not words, only sounds.*
*Nor do they really sing. They*
*screech, yodel, buzz, trumpet,*
*draw snot into their noses, smack*
*their lips, grunt, burp, ululate,*
*etc.: all of it in rhythm with the*
*song. Now they grow gradually*
*louder.*

None of the furniture may
catch dust
no hungry man may stand in
line
no adolescent may feel lust
everybody in his golden age
must feel fine
no flag may flutter in the
wrong direction
everybody belongs into his own
section

of town
every clown is out of luck
every word that doesn't mean
well must be struck.

*The Kaspars behind become
louder still. One of them unwraps
his package, the paper rustling
loudly in the process, takes a nail
file from the package and begins
filing his nails. Another Kaspar
repeats the process, rustling the
paper even more loudly and
taking an even bigger file out of
his package to file his nails with.
Filing noises can already be
heard.*

No elbow
on the table
no fish
with the knife
no sow
in the cable-
car
no kiss
for the wife
no truffles
uncooked
every bum in jail
muffle
all dissent.

*Kaspar is speaking again:*

No shit
on a real stick
no genuine finger
for a lick

*The prompters sing what Kaspar
utters, and the other Kaspars
squeak, bark, make the sounds of
rain and storm, blow up bubble
gum till it bursts, etc.*

every tit
in a snit
every fresh fish
for frying
every punctual plane
to depart on time
every real person
in the clear about everything
every healthy fruit
in the can
everything nonessential
down the drain.


64
*He stops speaking. There is*
*silence. Then Kaspar says:*

What was it
that
I said
just now?
If I only knew
what it is
that I said
just now!
If I only knew
what I said
just now!
What is that
that I said
just now?
What
was I
actually
saying
just now?
What was it
that was

being said
just now?
If I only knew
what I
said
just now!
What
was that
actually
that I was
saying
just now?

*Even while he is asking himself these questions, he, like the other Kaspars, begins to giggle and the like. At the same time the prompters sing his previous verses to the end. Kaspar, for instance, is snapping his finger against the microphone, producing a whine. All the Kaspars, while the prompters are singing, finally emit genuinely infectious laughter. Finally, sighing and giggling, the speaking Kaspar and the other Kaspars gradually grow quiet. The audience hears two or three of them filing their nails. Kaspar in front says:*
Every sentence
is for the birds
every sentence is for
the birds
every sentence is for the birds
*There is silence.*
*He begins to speak without versifying.*
*A spotlight is on him.*
I was proud of the first step I took, of the second step I felt ashamed; I was just as proud of the first hand which I discovered on myself, but of the second hand I felt ashamed: I felt ashamed of everything that I repeated; yet I felt ashamed even of the first sentence I uttered, whereas I no longer felt ashamed of the second sentence and soon became accustomed to the subsequent ones. I was proud of my second sentence.

In my story I only wanted to make a noise with my first sentence, whereas with my second sentence I wanted to call attention to myself, and I wanted to *speak* with the next sentence, and I wanted to *hear* myself *speak* with the next sentence, and with my next sentence I wanted *others* to hear my speaking, and with the next sentence I wanted others to hear *what* I said, and with the next sentence I wanted others who *also* uttered a sentence not to be heard, and used only the next to last sentence to *ask questions*, and began only with the last sentence of the story to ask what the *others* had said, the others who were ignored while I said my sentence.

I saw the snow and I touched the snow. Thereupon I said the sentence: I want to be someone like somebody else was once, with which I wanted to express why the snow was biting my hands. Once I woke up in the dark and saw nothing. Thereupon I said: I want to be someone like somebody else was once, with which I wanted to express, first of all, why is it that the whole room has been moved away, and then, because I did not see myself, why have I been cut off from everything that belongs to me, whereupon, because I had heard someone, namely myself, speaking, I said once more: I want to be someone like somebody else was once? – with which I wanted to express that I would have liked to have known who else was making fun of me while I was speaking. Then once I took a look into the open, where there was a very green glow, and I said to the open: I want to be someone like somebody else was once? – and with this sentence I wanted to ask the open why it was that my feet were aching. I also noticed a curtain that was moving. Thereupon I said, but not to the curtain: I want to be someone like somebody else was once, and with that I wanted to say, but not to the curtain, I don't know to whom, why are all the table drawers out and why does my coat always get caught in the door. I also heard someone climbing stairs which creaked, and thereupon I said to the creaking that I want to be someone like somebody else was once, with which I wanted to express when will my head feel lighter again. Once I also let my plate fall to the floor, but it did not break, whereupon I exclaimed: I want to be someone like somebody else was once, with which I meant that I was afraid of nothing in the world, whereupon I said once more: I want to be someone like somebody else was once, with which I wanted to make comprehensible that something probably could make me afraid, for example a cracked icicle; and once I felt no more pain, and I shouted: I want to be someone like somebody else was once, with which I wanted to say to everyone that I finally felt no more pain, but then I felt pain once more and I whispered in everyone's ear: I want to be someone like somebody else was once, with which I wanted to inform everyone that no, on the contrary, I felt no more pain and that everything was all right with me, with which I began to lie; and finally I said to myself: I want to be someone like somebody else was once, and wanted to know with that what that sentence, which I said to myself, what it actually means.

Because the snow was white and because snow was the first white I saw, I called everything white snow. I was given a handkerchief that was white, but I believed it would bite me because the white snow bit my hand when I touched it, and I did not touch the handkerchief, and when I knew the word snow I called the white handkerchief snow: but later, when I also knew the word handkerchief, when I saw a white handkerchief, even when I uttered the word handkerchief, I still thought the word snow, and then I first began to remember. But a brown or grey handkerchief was not snow, just as the first brown or grey snow I saw was not snow, but the first grey or brown that I saw, for example animal droppings or a sweater. But a white wall was snow, and just as much as absolutely everything became snow when I looked into the sun for a long time, because I then saw only snow. Finally I even used the word snow, out of curiosity, for something that was not white, to see whether it would turn to snow because of my uttering the word snow, and even if I did not say the word snow I was thinking it and remembered at every sight if not the snow itself at least the word snow. Even while falling asleep or while walking along a country lane or while running in the dark I kept saying the word snow all the time. But finally I reached the point where I no longer believed not only words and sentences about snow, but even the snow itself when it lay there in front of me or was falling, did not believe any more and held it neither for real nor as possible, only because I no longer believed the word snow.

The landscape at that time was a brightly coloured window shutter. As of the time that I saw the shadow a chair cast on the floor, I have from that time on always designated a fallen chair on the floor as the shadow of a chair. Each movement was running because at that time I wanted to do nothing but run and run away from everything; even swimming in the water was running. Jumping was running in the wrong direction. Even falling was running. Every liquid, even when it was calm, was a possible running. When I was afraid, the objects ran very quickly. But nightfall at that time was becoming unconscious.

When I did not know where to turn next, it was explained to me that I was afraid when I did not know where to turn, and that is how I learned to be afraid; and when I saw red it was explained to me that I was angry; but when I wanted to crawl away to hide I was ashamed; and when I leapt into the air I was happy; but when I was near bursting I had a secret or was proud of something; and when I nearly expired I had pity; but when I knew neither left nor right I was in despair: and when I did not know what was up or down I was confused; but when my breath stopped I was startled; and when I became ashen-faced I was afraid of death; but when I rubbed my hands together I was satisfied; and when I stuttered it was explained to me that I was happy when I stuttered; when I stuttered I was happy.

After I had learned to say the word I, I had to be addressed as I for a time because I did not know I was meant by the word you, since I was called I; and also, when I already knew the word you I pretended for a time that I did not know who was meant, because I enjoyed not understanding anything; thus I also began to enjoy responding whenever the word you was uttered.

When I did not understand a word I doubled it and doubled it once more, so that it would no longer bother me. I said: war, war; rag, rag. I said: war, war, war, war; rag, rag, rag, rag. Thus I became accustomed to words.

I first saw only one person. Later, after I had seen this one person, I saw several other persons.
That certainly surprised me.

*Meantime, one of the Kaspars has taken a large file out of his carton and rasped once across the carton. Thereupon he also begins to file on the Kaspar sitting next to him. The sound produced by the filing is of the kind that drives one wild. All the Kaspars wear some kind of material which, if a file, knife, or nail is applied to it, produces all manner of excruciating noises. Up to this point, only one of these noises has been produced, and briefly. The*

I saw something sparkle.
Because it sparkled, I wanted
to have it. I wanted to have
everything that sparkled. Later
I also wanted to have what
didn't sparkle.

I saw that someone had
something. I wanted to have
something like it. Later I also
wanted to have something.

When I woke up I ate. Then I
played and also spoke until I
fell asleep again and woke up
again.

Once I put my hands in my
pockets and could not pull
them out again.

Once every object seemed to
be evidence for something, but
what?

Once (*he tries to swallow*) I was
unable to swallow.

Once (*he tries to sneeze*) I was
unable to sneeze.

Once (*he tries to yawn*) I was
unable to yawn.

Once – (*with effort he tries to
speak the following sentence to
the end*) pursue the others . . .
I caught . . . no one vanquished
. . . the objects were . . . I
drove . . . no one caressed . . .
the others stormed . . . the
objects had . . . no one pushed
. . . I shoved . . . the others

*Kaspars might have on their
clothing pieces of foam rubber,
tin, stone, slate, etc. All these are
in the carton. One might also use
the noise produced by crumpling
the wrapping paper. The noises
now become increasingly more
frequent and louder because all
the Kaspars in back begin to
work on the cartons and on each
other with their files, knives,
slate pencils, nails, fingernails,
etc. One by one, they get up and
form a tight, wrangling huddle.
However, each noise is distinct
from the others: none is produced
indiscriminately; nor do they
drown out the words of the
original Kaspar at the
microphone; on the contrary,
they make them even more
distinct.*
*The sounds become increasingly
more ample and prolonged. For
instance, one will hear the sound
of a door scraping along a stone
floor, of a metal bar slipping
along a polar bear's claws in a
circus, of a sled running its
runners from snow on to gravel,
of chalk or a fingernail on slate,
of a knife scraping a plate, of
people scraping a marble floor
with nails in their shoes, of a saw
cutting through new wood, of a
fingernail scraping across a pane
of glass, of cloth tearing, etc.
(Leave something to the
imagination, but not too much.)*

showed . . . the objects became . . . I moved . . . the others ripped . . . no one lowered . . . the objects are . . . the objects have . . . the others rub . . . no one hits . . . I drag . . . the objects become . . . no one chokes . . . the others get . . . – I was unable to speak a sentence to the end.

*As these noises are produced, and as the various objects in the cartons (foam rubber, etc.) are cut up, the Kaspars gradually come to the front of the stage.*

Once made slip slip . . . once madip slip slip . . . once madip slin slin . . . monce mamin m:m:m . . . – I made a slip of the tongue, and they all looked at each other.

Once I was the only one who laughed.

Once I sat down on a fly.

Once I heard everyone scream murder! but when I looked I only found a peeled tomato in the rubbish bin.

All at once I was different from the furnishings.

Already with my first sentence I was trapped.

I can make myself understood. I think I must have slept a long time because I am awake now. I go to the table and use the table, but look at that – the table continues to exist after it has been used. I can appear because I know where my place is. I cannot fall asleep with dry hands, but when I spit into my hands they become even drier. By saying: the chair is harmless, it is all over with the chair's harmlessness. I feel good when the door, having stood open for long, is finally closed. I know where everything belongs. I have a good eye for the right proportion. I don't put anything into my mouth. I can laugh to three. I am usable. I can hear wood rotting over long distances. I no longer understand anything literally. I cannot wait until I wake up, whereas earlier I could not wait to fall asleep. I have been made to speak. I have been sentenced to reality. – Do you hear it? (*Silence.*) Can you hear? (*Silence.*) Psst. (*Silence.*)

*The stage becomes dark.*
*Silence.*

65
*As the stage becomes bright once more, the events on stage are again divided into three parts: together with Kaspar's speech as follows, the prompters come on again. Whispering, they repeat something like this: If only. Own future. Now every second one as opposed to every fourth one at one time. A possible object. If only. Make life easier. If only.* Development. If only. In reality. If only. In constantly growing numbers. If only. Serves the. If only. Bears dangers. If only. It is necessary for that. If only. *Finally, they repeat over and over again, until the end, speaking softly: If only. If only. If only. Meanwhile, the Kaspars come forward (filing, etc.) and proceed to manhandle the speaking Kaspar with their files, etc. They make particular fun of one object, say a chair, laughing at it, imitating it, costuming it, dragging it off and imitating the sound it makes as it is being dragged across the floor, thus making it utterly ridiculous and making it and all other objects* COMPLETELY IMPOSSIBLE. *Kaspar has gone on speaking:*

I can hear the logs comfortably crackling in the fire, with which I want to say that I do not hear the bones crackling comfortably. The chair stands here, the table there, with which I mean to say that I am telling a story. I would not like to be older, but I would like for much time to have passed, with which I mean to say that a sentence is a monster, with which I mean to say that speaking can help temporarily, with which I mean to say that every object becomes ticklish when I am startled. I say: I can imagine to be everywhere now, except that I cannot imagine really being there, with which I mean to say that the doorknobs are empty. I can say: the air snaps shut, or: the room creaks, or: the curtain jingles, with which I mean to say that I don't

97

know where I should put or leave my hand, while I when I say that I don't know where to put my hand mean to say that all doors tempt me under the pretence that they can be opened, which sentence I would like to use in the sense of: my hair has gotten into the table as into a machine and I am scalped: literally: with each new sentence I become nauseous: figuratively: I have been turned topsy-turvy: I am in someone's hand: I look to the other side: there prevails an unbloody calm: I cannot rid myself of myself any more: I toss the hat on to the meathook: every stool helps while dying: the furnishings are waterproof: the furniture is as it ought to be: nothing is open: the pain and its end come within sight: time must stop: thoughts become very small: I still experienced myself: I never saw myself: I put up no undue resistance: the shoes fit like gloves: I don't get away with just a fright: the skin peels off: the foot sleeps itself dead: candles and bloodsuckers: ice and mosquitoes: horses and puss: hoarfrost and rats: eels and sicklebills:

*Meantime, the other Kaspars are producing an infernal noise with their various tools which they have applied to the objects they have brought with them and to Kaspar. They are giggling, behave like crowds in crowd scenes in plays, ridicule Kaspar by speaking in the same rhythm as he, etc. Kaspar has also produced a file and makes similar noises by scraping with the file against the microphone while he is speaking his sentences. But now, all at once, an almost complete silence sets in. The Kaspars merely flap their arms about a little and gesticulate. They wriggle a little. They snuffle. Then Kaspar says:*

| Goats and monkeys | *With that, the curtain jolts a little towards the centre, where the Kaspars are wriggling. The jolt produces a shrill sound.* |
| Goats and monkeys | *With an even shriller sound, the curtain jerks a little farther towards the middle.* |
| Goats and monkeys | *With an even shriller sound, the curtain jerks still farther towards the middle.* |

| | |
|---|---|
| Goats and monkeys | *With an even shriller sound, the curtain moves still more towards the centre.* |
| Goats and monkeys | *With the shrillest possible sound, the curtain makes one final jerk towards the centre, where the Kaspars are still wriggling a little. The curtain slams into them the moment Kaspar says his last word: it topples all of them. They fall over, but fall behind the curtain, which has now come together. The piece is over.* |

# Methuen's Modern Plays

EDITED BY JOHN CULLEN

| | |
|---|---|
| Paul Ableman | *Green Julia* |
| Jean Anouilh | *Antigone* |
| | *Becket* |
| | *Poor Bitos* |
| | *Ring Round the Moon* |
| | *The Lark* |
| | *The Rehearsal* |
| | *The Fighting Cock* |
| | *Dear Antoine* |
| John Arden | *Serjeant Musgrave's Dance* |
| | *The Workhouse Donkey* |
| | *Armstrong's Last Goodnight* |
| | *Left-handed Liberty* |
| | *Soldier, Soldier and other plays* |
| | *Two Autobiographical plays* |
| John Arden and Margaretta D'Arcy | *The Business of Good Government* |
| | *The Royal Pardon* |
| | *The Hero Rises Up* |
| Ayckbourn, Bowen, Brook, Campton, Melly, Owen, Pinter, Saunders, Weldon | *Mixed Doubles* |
| Brendan Behan | *The Quare Fellow* |
| | *The Hostage* |
| Barry Bermange | *No Quarter* and *The Interview* |
| Edward Bond | *Saved* |
| | *Narrow Road to the Deep North* |
| | *The Pope's Wedding* |
| John Bowen | *Little Boxes* |
| | *The Disorderly Women* |
| Bertolt Brecht | *Mother Courage* |
| | *The Caucasian Chalk Circle* |
| | *The Good Person of Szechwan* |
| | *The Life of Galileo* |
| Syd Cheatle | *Straight Up* |
| Shelagh Delaney | *A Taste of Honey* |
| | *The Lion In Love* |
| Max Frisch | *The Fire Raisers* |
| | *Andorra* |

\*    \*    \*

# Methuen Playscripts

\*    \*    \*

# Methuen's Theatre Classics